L'ASSOMMOIR

Borgo Press Books by WILLIAM BUSNACH

L'Assommoir (with Émile Zola)
Mathias Sandorf (with Jules Verne)

L'ASSOMMOIR

A PLAY IN FIVE ACTS

ÉMILE ZOLA &

WILLIAM BUSNACH

Translated and Adapted by Frank J. Morlock

THE BORGO PRESS
MMXIII

L'ASSOMMOIR

Copyright © 2002, 2013 by Frank J. Morlock

FIRST BORGO PRESS EDITION

Published by Wildside Press LLC

www.wildsidebooks.com

DEDICATION

For Bea Aaronson and Dagny,
who don't know each other,
but are Zola enthusiasts

CONTENTS

CAST OF CHARACTERS	9
ACT I, Scene 1 (1851)	11
ACT I, Scene 2	27
ACT II, Scene 3 (1851)	41
ACT II, Scene 4	62
ACT III, Scene 5 (1858)	96
ACT III, Scene 6	118
ACT IV, Scene 7 (1860)	152
ACT V, Scene 8 (1868)	177
ACT V, Scene 9	199
ABOUT THE AUTHOR	213

CAST OF CHARACTERS

COUPEAU

LANTIER

MES-BOTTES

GOUGET

POISSON, former soldier

BIBI LA GRILLADE

BEC-SALE

LORILLEUX

BAZOUGE

MADINIER

PÈRE COLOMBE

ADOLPH, waiter in a restaurant

CHARLES

ZIDORE

UGENE, a kid

GERVAISE

VIRGINIA

MADAME GOUGET

MADAME LORILLEUX

MADAME BOCHE

ADULT NANA

AUGUSTINE

CLEMENCE

MADAME PUTOIS

JULIETTE

CATHERINE

LOUISE

YOUNG NANA

A LITTLE GIRL

ACT I (1851)
SCENE 1

The Hotel Boncoeur. A furnished room in the hotel. To the left a window. In the back a bed, then a door. To the right a chimney, further back a commode. Washing furniture.

Gervaise is alone.

At rise, she looks through the window, then turns back.

GERVAISE

No! It's still not him. Where can he be? All night I've waited for him without budging from this place. Oh! I've got a fever! Yesterday evening, he left telling me he was going to look for work. And it seemed to me, I saw him entering the dance at the Grand Balcony. Behind him, I thought I noticed Virginia, the hat maker, walking five or six steps, hands balled up, as if she'd just let his arm go, so as not to pass together in front of my door. Perhaps I didn't see right. (she again looks through the window) Still nothing!

MADAME BOCHE (entering)

Hello, Madame Lantier.

GERVAISE (turning)

Ah! It's you, Madame Boche!

MADAME BOCHE

You're taking the air at a fine hour. It's still a little brisk this morning. And Mr. Lantier, has he already left?

GERVAISE (embarrassed)

Yes. He had a meeting with a master—about some business.

MADAME BOCHE (aside)

That's just as I thought. He hasn't returned.

(aloud)

Ah! Hell! When you're in business, you are not master of your time. That's what I always say to Boche who wants to thrust himself into industry. I say to him, "Let's remain concierges. We have a nice lodging and the tips bring us enough to offer us comforts." The only disagreeable thing is that we can't go out together in company: one of the two of us must always be on duty. And I'm the one who goes out. (seeing Gervaise still looking out the window) But what are you looking like that for in the street? Has something happened?

GERVAISE

No, Madame Boche.

MADAME BOCHE (aside)

For sure, she's hiding her problem! (aloud) This is the morning that you are going to wash, right?

GERVAISE

Yes, indeed.

MADAME BOCHE

Me, too. I will keep a place by my side and we will jaw a little.

GERVAISE

Certainly, with pleasure, Madame Boche.

MADAME BOCHE (seeing Gervaise go back to the window)

Say there, my little friend, you'd do better not to stay there. You'll catch cold.

COUPEAU (putting his head through the door)

Can I come in?

GERVAISE

Come in, of course, Mr. Coupeau.

COUPEAU

I'm not disturbing you, neighbor—coming down the stairway to go to work—I saw your key in your door. Then, I said to myself: I'm going to say good day to my neighbor as a friend. Huh! This morning is brisk.

MADAME BOCHE

Isn't it? That's what I was telling, Madame Lantier. Shut your window. (to Coupeau) And what's new in the neighborhood?

COUPEAU

My word, you're asking in the wrong place! In the morning I go to my bosses' place, I come back at night—my day's over at once. Then, after having eaten I go to bed and stay there until the next day.

GERVAISE

That's true, Mr. Coupeau. You are a fine worker, indeed! You work!

COUPEAU

Hell! I've got arms. They're to be put to use! Work doesn't frighten me. I don't get melancholy, and I haven't time to be bored.

MADAME BOCHE

That's just like me. But I am late. Till later, Madame Lantier. Your servant, Mr. Coupeau. (she leaves)

COUPEAU (seeing Gervaise is sad)

What's wrong with you this morning, Madame Gervaise? The boss isn't here?

GERVAISE (somber)

No.

COUPEAU

He went out before daybreak?

GERVAISE

Yes. (bursts into tears) Ah, I am indeed wretched!

COUPEAU

Look, look, what's the matter?

GERVAISE

It's that—Lantier didn't come home last night. I spent the night at this window waiting for him and crying.

COUPEAU

My God, you mustn't be desolated. You know, Lantier's very busy with politics. Indeed, perhaps he remained with friends—to speak ill of the government—that distracts him! A wife must be indulgent with her husband.

GERVAISE (exploding)

My husband! Would he dare to behave in this way if I were his wife?

COUPEAU

What, you aren't?

GERVAISE

Listen, Mr. Coupeau, I am going to tell you everything. Perhaps you will give me some good advice. No—I am not his wife. My God! This happens, this happens all the time. The two of us are from Plassans, a town in Midi. Ah, I wasn't very happy! For a yes, for a no, my father, old man Macquart as he was known, would kick me in the ass—you had to see it! So then, right? You think of taking a bit of good times outside—I knew Lantier since my childhood. He was the son of a neighbor. I was sixteen. He was twenty. And then, and then—

COUPEAU

He didn't behave properly with you?

GERVAISE

Don't mention it to me. He was sweet to me at Plassans, but after we left the country I can no long get to the end of it. I have to tell you that his mother died last year, leaving him nearly seven hundred francs. He wanted to leave for Paris. Then as papa Macquart was still sending me blows without warning, I consented to go with him. He was to set me up as a washerwoman and work in his trade of hatter. We ought to have been very happy. But, you see, Lantier is ambitious, a spender, a man who only thinks of his own amusement. In the last analysis he's not worth much.

COUPEAU

Poor Madame Gervaise.

GERVAISE

After arriving in Paris we stayed at a hotel in Montmartre and then there were carriages, the theatre, a watch for him, a dress for me, for he doesn't have a bad heart when he has money. So much so that at the end of two months we were soaked. It was then that we came to live here—this Boulevard de la Chapelle, at the Hotel Boncoeur—and that my unhappiness began.

COUPEAU

Go on. Perhaps you are exaggerating.

GERVAISE

Oh! No! I see clearly what he's doing. Lantier no longer loves me.

COUPEAU

No longer loves you? You—a little woman, so sweet, so devoted!

GERVAISE

I am sure he's in love with someone else. That big Virginia, perhaps!

COUPEAU

Now there are some ideas! Where could he find a woman who's worth you? Look, calm down! I am going to look for him and I'll bring him back to you even if I have to search the four corners of Paris.

GERVAISE

What about your work?

COUPEAU

Indeed, one can sacrifice a few hours for friends. Don't be desolate, I beg you. You are causing me too much pain. Ah, if you knew (taking her hand, looking at her very moved) Till later, Madame Gervaise. (he leaves very excitedly)

GERVAISE (alone)

What a brave lad. If Lantier resembled him! Let's try to be calm. Let's wait for him while doing my housework. (she tries to straighten things up) But where did he spend the night? And that Virginia who was following him—for it was she I saw entering the Grand Balcony! My head's spinning! Impossible to work (weeping) My God, what have I done to have so much trouble like this? (going to the window) I still think I hear him. (Gervaise is at the window. Lantier enters without her noticing him. He throws his hat on the chest in a gesture of ill humor. Gervaise sees him and rushes towards him)

GERVAISE

You! It's you!

LANTIER (brutally pushing her away)

Well, yes, it's me! What's wrong with you?

GERVAISE

What's wrong with me?

LANTIER

You're not going to start your stupidities, are you?

GERVAISE

Is this reasonable? In what uneasiness you've put me! I didn't shut my eyes. I thought something bad had happened to you.

Where did you go? Where did you spend the night? My God, don't start over. I will go crazy. Look, tell me, where did you go?

LANTIER (shrugging his shoulders)

Yes, by Jove, I had business. I was at the home of this friend who's going to set up a hat factory. I was late—so I preferred to sleep there. You know I don't like anyone to annoy me. Leave me alone.

GERVAISE (weeping)

My God! My God!

LANTIER (furious)

Ah! Now there's the music I was expecting! Listen, if this continues, I'm out of here. And for good and all this time. You don't intend to shut up? That's fine, I'll return from where I came.

GERVAISE

No, no. It's over, I won't weep any more. (changing tone) Yesterday evening, I saw Madame Fauconnier, the washerwoman of the Rue de la Neuve. She will take me tomorrow. And you? Are you soon going to work?

LANTIER (stretched out on the bed)

To work—work—I ask for nothing better but you'd say it doesn't cling to me, work. I don't find any.

GERVAISE (getting carried away)

Yes, I know love of work doesn't choke you. You are croaking with ambition. You want to dress like a gentleman and promenade with women in silk skirts.

LANTIER (furious)

Gervaise!

GERVAISE

You haven't found me quite swank enough since I put all my dresses in pawn at Mont de Piété! Heavens, Lantier, I don't want to mention it to you, I would have kept on waiting. But I know where you spent the night. I saw you go into the Grand Balcony with Virginia. Ah, you pick 'em good! She's right to take on the airs of a princess, that one!

(Lantier rises and, controlling the desire to beat her, seizes her and shakes her violently. She falls into a chair.)

LANTIER

Gervaise, you don't know what you just did. You will see!

GERVAISE

Ah! You hurt me! (she weeps silently; then, after a moment of silence, she rises, makes a package of linen without saying anything)

LANTIER

What are you doing? Where are you going? (Gervaise does not reply) I'm asking you where you are going?

GERVAISE

You can see plainly. I'm going to wash, that's all.

LANTIER

That's good. Say, Gervaise, do you have any money?

GERVAISE

Where do you think I would have stolen money? You know very well that they loaned me three francs day before yesterday against my black skirt. We've lunched twice on it. No, no doubt, I don't have any money. I've got four sou left for the wash. As for me, I don't make money like certain women.

LANTIER (after having looked everywhere, unhooks a trousers and a shawl)

Here, take that to pawn.

GERVAISE

That's all we've got left.

LANTIER

Don't worry. (seeing that Gervaise remains motionless) And pretend you don't know where the pawn shop is.

GERVAISE

Oh! Yes! I've been down that road often enough during the last month. It's only two steps, in the house on the side. I'll be back right away. You haven't kissed me.

LANTIER

Stupidities. (kisses her) Don't linger.

GERVAISE (aside)

Perhaps I'm mistaken after all. (she leaves)

LANTIER (alone)

Come on, come on—mustn't hesitate any more, got to end this existence! We got together because we agreed. When you no longer agree, got to part and that's all there is to it. (turns toward suitcase and starts to pack)

COUPEAU (entering excitedly)

Madame Gervaise—they told me you met (noticing Lantier) Ah, you are there! That's nice! I've been chasing after you for an hour.

LANTIER (turning)

After me. Why's that?

COUPEAU (seeing Lantier pack his trunk)

What's that you're doing?

LANTIER

Nothing. Straightening up my linen.

COUPEAU

Then, you've seen your wife?

LANTIER

No doubt, I've seen her.

COUPEAU

She was very sad, very worried.

LANTIER

Ah! She told you.

COUPEAU

You want to know what I say, Lantier? It's not right for you to hurt Gervaise who loves you so much.

LANTIER

Look here, you! Are you going to bore me with your moralizing? Meddle with what concerns you.

(Gervaise enters without seeing Coupeau)

GERVAISE

Here's all they gave me. Four francs. I tried to get five for it. There was no way.

LANTIER (abruptly)

That's good. Put that on the chimney.

COUPEAU (aside)

They're at it!

GERVAISE (noticing Coupeau)

Ah, Mr. Coupeau, I didn't see you. (to Lantier) While I'm at the washhouse you will go find something for lunch.

LANTIER

Yes! Yes!

GERVAISE (heading towards the trunk)

I'm going to take your linen.

LANTIER

No. It's not necessary.

GERVAISE

But, it really still needs—

LANTIER (snatching the linen from her and hurling it in the trunk)

Damnation! Obey me for once! If I tell you to leave it alone!

COUPEAU (trying to calm him)

Lantier!

LANTIER

It's not about Lantier! She must obey!

GERVAISE (uneasy)

Why don't you want me to take your linen as I usually do?

LANTIER (embarrassed)

Why? Why? You are going to say everywhere that you're busy with me. Well, that bores me! Do your business, I will do mine. Go to the wash!

GERVAISE

That's good. (aside) He's got bad ideas for certain. (she leaves, making a sign of goodbye to Coupeau)

(Hardly has Gervaise closed the door than Lantier finishes packing the truck)

LANTIER

At last! That's not bad!

COUPEAU (surprised)

What is it you're doing?

LANTIER

What am I doing? I am changing my residence.

COUPEAU

Huh?

LANTIER

I've had enough of this hell. I am resuming my life as a bachelor.

COUPEAU

You're abandoning Gervaise?

LANTIER

A bit, my nephew! Let's see, I'm not forgetting anything. (he looks around) That, that's mine. (stops before the money) Bah! Since she's working with her washerwoman tomorrow. (puts the money in his pocket, then looks out the window) There are some cabs on the square. En route! (leaving the trunk on the landing) You can deliver her her key. Here! With a real goodbye on my part.

COUPEAU (following him)

Lantier! Lantier! You can't possibly be doing this.

LANTIER (gaily)

Goodbye old boy. One of these days. (he leaves)

COUPEAU (alone)

Ah! Evil heart! To drag a woman who loves you from the end of France and leave her without a penny on the pavements of Paris! The police ought to pick up men like that! That poor Gervaise, I don't have the heart to announce it to her myself, I would weep with her! I'm going to have her key sent to her. She will understand. (leaves and shuts the door)

CURTAIN

ACT I
SCENE 2

A large washhouse at La Chapelle. A vast hangar with large empty bays. Rows of wash pails to the right and left.

At Rise, a great uproar. Songs and the noise of beating.

CATHERINE

Where'd I put my soap? They've taken my soap again.

LOUISE

Give me the soda.

MADAME BOCHE (at the right, near the audience)

But, where's Charles the washboy? (calling) Charles! Charles! (seeing him arrive) Finally, that's lucky.

CHARLES

What do you want, Madame Boche?

MADAME BOCHE

A pail of hot water and fast.

JULIETTE (laughing)

Especially, don't think about drinking it on the way.

CATHERINE

Oh, it's not with water that he freshens up.

MADAME BOCHE

What a barracks this wash place is! When you don't need a thing, you get immediate service.

JULIETTE and CATHERINE (singing at the left)

Boom, boom, boom,
Margay's doing the wash!
Boom, boom, boom, the wash is beaten.
Boom, boom, boom, go wash his heart
Boom, boom, boom, all filthy with sorrow!

CHARLES (bringing a pail of hot water to Madame Boche)

That's your water. It's a sou.

MADAME BOCHE (giving him a sou)

Here, my lad. By the way, you know I'm keeping a place for a neighbor girl who's going to come. Oh! There she is now! (seeing Gervaise enter, calling) Over here, my little friend.

GERVAISE

Thanks, Madame Boche.

MADAME BOCHE

Put yourself there. (Gervaise opens her box) Your pack is quite small! Before noon we will have finished that and we can go to lunch. You're not taking a bucket of lye water?

GERVAISE (meanwhile has pulled out her linen)

Oh. Hot water is fine. It knows me.

MADAME BOCHE

It knows you, huh? You were a washerwoman in your country?

GERVAISE (rolling up her sleeves and beating her linen)

Yes, yes, a washerwoman at ten years old. Eight years since then We went to the river. Ah, it was much nicer than here. There was a spot under the trees with clear running water. (she stops beating) The water is hard in Paris.

MADAME BOCHE

That's not surprising, from agreement with the population. As I left you just now, I met Mr. Lantier on the street.

GERVAISE

Yes, he came back. Heavens! I forgot my blue.

MADAME BOCHE

Don't disturb yourself. I have some at your service.

GERVAISE

Thanks.

MADAME BOCHE

Between you and me, I think he's a bit of a chaser.

GERVAISE (emotionally)

Lantier! What do you mean?

MADAME BOCHE

Why, I don't know anything, or at least nothing much. Virginia—indeed, you know that big Virginia, my tenant.

GERVAISE (more and more uneasy)

Yes! Well?

MADAME BOCHE

Well, every time he meets her, he jokes with her.

GERVAISE (exploding)

I'm not mistaken. It was with Virginia he went last night to the Grand Balcony.

MADAME BOCHE (very lit up)

To the Grand Balcony, you saw them. (aside) So that's it. (aloud) Ah, my little friend, you are deceiving yourself. He jokes with her but it never goes farther than that—my word of honor!

GERVAISE

Ah! That girl! If I was sure! If I was sure!

(Virginia enters)

MADAME BOCHE

Heavens! Speak of the Devil! There she is, Virginia! What's she come to wash here with her four knots in her handkerchief?

GERVAISE (looking at her)

She! It's she!

VIRGINIA (to Charles)

Do you have a spot?

CHARLES

Down there to the right.

JULIETTE

Over this way, Virginia!

VIRGINIA (going to the left)

Yes there. I'll be very fine there.

MADAME BOCHE (to Gervaise)

Now there's a caprice. She's never soaped a pair of gloves! A famous pretender. I'll wager for that. A dress maker who doesn't mend anything except her boots.

VIRGINIA (noticing Madame Boche)

It's you, Madame Boche. Are you well this morning?

MADAME BOCHE

See for yourself. (low to Gervaise who's looking at Virginia fixedly) Look, don't stare at her like that, you're going to cause a scandal. Here the two of you devour each other with your eyes. Since I tell you there's nothing to it!

GERVAISE

I don't want her to look at me.

MADAME BOCHE

Be reasonable! I'm going to help you twist your linen—and we will leave.

(they both twist linen)

GERVAISE

Yes, yes, quick or I won't answer for myself.

CHARLES (entering)

Madame Lantier!

GERVAISE

What's the matter?

CHARLES

A kid's asking for you.

GERVAISE

What's he want with me?

MADAME BOCHE (seeing Ugene enter)

Heaves! It's Ugene—the little boy of your landlord Mr. Madinier.

UGENE

Hello, Madame Lantier. Here's what Mr. Coupeau ordered me to deliver to you. (delivers the key)

GERVAISE

My key? Why's he bringing me my key?

UGENE

Hell! I don't know. It's for you to know.

GERVAISE

My God! What's it mean?

VIRGINIA

Really (laughing) it's not difficult to comprehend!

UGENE (with a wink)

Mr. Lantier left.

GERVAISE

Left! But he's going to return?

UGENE

Oh! I don't think so. I saw him get in a cab with his trunk.

GERVAISE

Left! So that was it! Ah! My God! Ah! My God! (she bursts into tears)

UGENE

My errand's performed. I'm off. (he runs out)

MADAME BOCHE (to Gervaise)

Come on, come on, my little friend, courage!

VIRGINIA (laughing)

Ah! Ha! (she chokes her laughter)

MADAME BOCHE

Be reasonable! Everyone's looking at you. Is it possible to make oneself so much trouble over a man? How stupid we women are!

GERVAISE

No! Such an abomination has never been seen!

MADAME BOCHE

The fact is he's a rough customer! A pretty little woman like you! Now, can I tell you everything?

GERVAISE

Yes, speak, speak.

MADAME BOCHE

Well! With this Virginia—I've known about it for a long while. Last night, they came back together.

GERVAISE (no longer weeping, looking at Virginia)

Last night! And there I was waiting at the window.

VIRGINIA (to the washerwoman)

Damn! After all, when you've had enough of a woman, right? (she laughs)

MADAME BOCHE

She's laughing. The heartless—I will bet her washing is only a pretext. She's come here to talk her head off about what you would do.

GERVAISE

That's fine, thanks. You're going to see. (she takes a pail of soapy water, goes toward Virginia and throws it at her) Here! This is for you!

VIRGINIA (who jumped back and didn't receive the water)

Well! What's gotten into you—to rage here. Come forward a bit so we can see you. You, you don't have to come put on the swank with us here. As for me, did I know! If she'd—she had caught me, you ought to have seen this. What's she say that I did to her? Speak—what was done to you?

GERVAISE (through her teeth)

Don't talk so much! You know very well you were seen last night with my husband. And shut up, because you're going to have a bad time, I swear to you.

VIRGINIA

Her husband! Ah! She's bold, she is! Madame's husband! As if one had husbands with this gimp. It's not my fault, if he left you. You can search me, I didn't steal him.

(laughter from the washerwomen)

GERVAISE

Wretch!

VIRGINIA

So—you lost your man! Did he have his collar on at least? Who's found Madame's husband? There's an honest reward!

(laughter increases)

GERVAISE

You know very well! You know very well! I will strangle you.

VIRGINIA (bluntly)

Well, yes! I took him from you! Are you satisfied? The two of us will adore him together. And he let you go. He had enough of you!

GERVAISE (pulling stuff from a small pail and throwing the contents on her)

Slut!

VIRGINIA

She ruined my dress! Wait, wait— (she throws the water from her pail) You caught that one. Brush your teeth in it!

(the washerwomen separate them and restrain them)

JULIETTE

They're not funny!

LOUISE

She's right—the blonde—if she took her husband from her.

MADAME BOCHE (who has prudently withdrawn)

I have palpitations. Charles! Charles!

CHARLES (peeping)

Oh! What a farce! What a farce!

MADAME BOCHE

What? There you are. Go find the cops!

CHARLES

No, no! That would compromise the house.

GERVAISE (to the washerwomen holding her back)

Let me go, let me do her business!

VIRGINIA (taking her stick)

Ah. Madame wants the great—

GERVAISE

Don't laugh—it's necessary that one of the two of us remain. (taking her stick) Ah—I'll mark you for the rest of your life. Here!

(the washerwomen watch the two combatants. Charles standing on a chair, roars in laughter)

THE WASHERWOMEN

They're going to kill each other, separate them.

VIRGINIA (letting out a scream)

Ah!

GERVAISE (coming out of the circle)

She got what was coming to her.

(the group opens. Virginia withdraws to the right, all ashamed)

MADAME BOCHE (to Gervaise)

My God! What butchery! Let's get out of here right away. Do you want me to help you? (she throws her wet linen over her shoulder)

GERVAISE

Thanks!

LOUISE

A plucky woman, all the same—the blonde!

THEWASHERWOMEN

Bravo! Bravo!

GERVAISE (returning to Virginia)

And don't swagger or I'll start over. (she withdraws)

THE WASHERWOMEN

Bravo! Bravo!

VIRGINIA (alone—forestage)

Let her remember today. As for me, I'll never forget it. And I'll avenge myself, even if I have to die to do it. (shaking her fist) You've just made your misfortune.

ALL THE WOMEN

Bravo! Bravo!

(Gervaise is on the steps at the back. She turns one last time to look at Virginia)

CURTAIN

ACT II (1851)
SCENE 3

The Poissionière Barricade. The street of Poissionière at the corner of the Boulevard Rocherhovant. To the left Père Colombe's Dram Shop. To the right, the Bomerade. Tax collectors at the grilled gate.

AT RISE, the stage is empty. It's early morning. The shops have just opened, lit by the rosy reflection of gas. A waiter places two tables and four iron chairs in front of the Dram Shop. A mason appears from the left, crosses the stage, blowing on his fingers. He's got half a loaf of bread under his arm. After that several passers-by are seen. Little by little the workers come down to their work. locksmiths having blue aprons, painters with coveralls under which they place white shirts. A worker stops to light his pipe then moves on. Daylight increases, the lights in the shop are extinguished. Bibi la Grillade and Bec-Sale enter in the midst of a wave of workers who become fewer.

BIBI

Look, Bec-Sale! Keep on going, we will be late getting to the workyard.

BEC-SALE

You're fine, you are, Bibi. You aren't tired. As for me, I can't do anymore.

BIBI

What's wrong with you?

BEC-SALE

I don't know. I think it's nerves.

BIBI

Nerves! These nerves'll serve you. Admit that you've got an aversion to work.

BEC-SALE

Maybe so. And you?

BIBI

I am not disposed that way anymore.

BEC-SALE

I've got to push Mes-Bottes out of the nest. Doubtless we'll see him come to the Dram Shop soon enough.

BIBI

Probable! Ah, he's a bold character, Mes-Bottes. The King of Bunglers, one might say. And dapper.

BEC-SALE

Shall we go in and wait for him?

BIBI

What? Are you paying?

BEC-SALE

Ah, as for that! Fuck! The stars are touching, my old chum. (pulling out his pockets)

(Coupeau watches the rear of the stage)

BIBI

Heck! There's Coupeau! Suppose we were to invite him?

BEC-SALE

And the cash?

BIBI

You're dumb. If we were to invite him—he has to offer us something.

BEC-SALE

Joker, go! There's no danger that he'll buy a round that joker.

BIBI

But what's he do—to pose like that?

BEC-SALE

Haven't you noticed the last couple of weeks? He comes to look at the one he's sweet on!

BIBI

Go on! G'wan!

BEC-SALE

Here—to prove it!

GERVAISE (entering briskly)

Seven o'clock. Madame Fauconnier is going to scold me, most certainly.

COUPEAU (calling her)

Madame Gervaise! Madame Gervaise!

GERVAISE

Ah, it's you, Mr. Coupeau!

COUPEAU

I have to speak to you.

GERVAISE

No, no, I'm late. Later, if you like. I will come back this way when I bring the wash to the customers.

COUPEAU

Madame Gervaise, I beg you. (disappears behind her)

BEC-SALE

Right! Say, then, you know about Lantier—he broke up with Virginia. He advised her to marry a youngster by name of Poisson who's paying court to her.

BIBI

I know him, Poisson. A former soldier who wants to become a cop.

BEC-SALE

Exactly.

BIBI

Funny taste.

BEC-SALE

Ah, that doesn't attract the women—with this pretty head of Lantier's. Now there's Coupeau who's going to inherit the blonde, and there's Poisson who's getting the brunette. As for him, he remains a bachelor so he can feast in other households.

BIBI

Meanwhile we're dying of thirst.

BEC-SALE

And not one round of drinks.

BIBI

All the same, let's go into Père Colombe's.

BEC-SALE

Got to try to soften him up. I asked him if he'd open a credit account for us.

BIBI

You haven't enough even to pay,

BEC-SALE

And what about my signature?

BIBI

Heavens, that's a plan! We'll propose signing a note to him.

(They go into the dram shop.)

(A new wave of people crosses the stage. Mostly workers. They come in groups of two or three. Then one sees employees coming, eating a loaf of bread and moving quickly.)

COUPEAU (entering)

She promised me to come back. I absolutely must speak to her. This can't go on like this. I love her too much.

MES-BOTTES (enters, singing, a bit drunk)

Autumn sun
Gilds our scythes,

Come on, my pretty,
Open your curtains.

COUPEAU (aside, bothered)

Right. There's Mes-Bottes.

MES-BOTTES

Heavens! That aristo of Cadet Cassis! A gentleman who smokes with paper and who has some linen! You intend then to flabbergast your acquaintances.

COUPEAU

Ah! You know! Leave me in peace!

MES-BOTTES

We're not annoyed. Come, I'll buy a round.

COUPEAU

No, I'm going to—

MES-BOTTES

Thanks! Excuse me! No More of this stuff. Ah, indeed, as for me, if they wanted me at the barricades today, the sub-master can indeed come looking for me. Go in, I'll buy a round.

COUPEAU

No!

MES-BOTTES

Now there's a greenhorn! Wretch! That one thinks he's a good worker and he trembles before a pick-me-up?

(Gervaise appears.)

COUPEAU (aside)

Gervaise!

MES-BOTTES

Bye, bye, Cadet Cassis. It's all the same, it's not nice to refuse a friend. (noticing Gervaise) Ah! Right! Ah! Indeed! (heading toward the dram shop) That you are sipping in down there. It's the hope of Spring. It's a mother's passion. (to Gervaise) Hello, Madame. (resumes singing)

Children, don't touch it!

(goes into the dram shop)

(Gervaise has a big basket of linen under her arm)

COUPEAU (aside)

At last! (aloud) That's Mes-Comrade—a comrade. Got to excuse him, he bends the elbow a bit.

GERVAISE

Your name's Cadet Cassis, Mr. Coupeau?

COUPEAU

Oh, a surname they've given me because I generally take a liquor when friends lead me by force to the wine merchant. No more named Cadet Cassis than Mes-Bottes, right?

GERVAISE

For sure. That's not nasty—Cadet Cassis. (at this moment one hears bawling singing from the dram shop) (she turns) That frightens me, places like that I get a little shiver when I pass by. A man who drinks is capable of anything.

COUPEAU

I never drink, Madame Gervaise, you know that quite well.

GERVAISE

If you drank, I wouldn't speak to you.

COUPEAU

Oh, there's no danger. The comrades waste their time joking with me. You see, Papa Coupeau who had the same profession I do broke his head in a fall from a gutter one day of drunkenness and that memory in our family made us cautious. I don't know how they can swallow full glasses of brandy.

GERVAISE

Brandy is the curse of poor folk. I've known so many women who wept!

COUPEAU (very gallant)

As for me, I wouldn't make you weep.

GERVAISE

No doubt. You're as gay as a lark.

COUPEAU

Oh! You understand me well enough Madame Gervaise.

GERVAISE

What about?

COUPEAU

Would you—?

(he tries to put his arm about her waist)

GERVAISE

What? Are you still singing that old song?

COUPEAU

Why, always, Madame Gervaise.

GERVAISE (gaily)

Look, you aren't going to start your silliness all over again. I've told you, no.

COUPEAU

When women say no, sometimes that means yes.

GERVAISE

Be reasonable or I'm going to get angry. As for me, I am all alone in life. Necessarily, I must think of serious things. My misfortune has been a real lesson. I don't want to start over again.

COUPEAU (still trying)

You can indeed laugh. We would be so sweet, the two of us together. We'd laugh.

GERVAISE

Exactly, I no longer want to laugh like that. I have lots of work, I don't need anyone. Oh, I don't say it couldn't happen! You are a good lad—you don't cause sadness. Only it doesn't please me. I prefer to stay as I am, to earn my bread and eat it peacefully.

COUPEAU (anxiously)

In that case, no?

GERVAISE

No, for sure.

COUPEAU

Never?

GERVAISE (laughing and wanting to go)

In a week full of Mondays.

COUPEAU (stopping her)

Madame Gervaise, I beg you. Wait a short moment. You are causing me pain, a great deal of pain. You see it chokes me up, twists me.

GERVAISE (touched)

I do see. But what can I do? It's not possible.

COUPEAU

I love you, I love you so I'm no longer able to work. The tools fall from my hands. I stay there on the roofs looking at distant chimneys smoking. This cannot continue. I will fall ill.

GERVAISE

Calm down, Mr. Coupeau. If you could see yourself gesticulating.

COUPEAU

Don't go. I have something to tell you. Here, let's sit down a moment. (he points to the place before the Dram Shop) We'll have something—whatever you like. A plum cocktail?

GERVAISE

Come on, I'm really glad to, so as not to upset you. (they sit in front of the Dram Shop)

COUPEAU

Waiter. (the waiter comes) Two plums. (the waiter goes back. Coupeau lets out a big sigh)

GERVAISE

Ah! My God, what's wrong with you?

COUPEAU

Madame Gervaise, I have something here—and it weighs very heavy.

GERVAISE

Is it that serious? (the waiter returns with the two drinks. Coupeau pays.)

COUPEAU (in a deep, profound voice)

Madame Gervaise, we are going to get married.

GERVAISE (stupefied)

We're going to get married?

COUPEAU

Yes—I mean it.

GERVAISE

Oh! Mr. Coupeau, what are you looking for there? You know quite well I've never asked you to marry me. That doesn't suit me, that's all.

COUPEAU

I see it.

GERVAISE

No. This is getting serious. Consider, now, I beg you.

COUPEAU

The whole thing's considered. Say yes and I won't torture you anymore.

GERVAISE

Indeed, I won't say yes like that! I don't intend for you to accuse me later of having pushed you to do something stupid. (lowering her eyes) Indeed, you know that.

COUPEAU (excitedly, with passion)

I know that nowhere will I find a better wife—full of qualities or more pretty. With one word you can make my happiness or my misery. Say yes.

GERVAISE (disturbed)

I assure you, we would likely repent. You have a family.

COUPEAU

I don't have to give an account to my sister nor to my brother-in-law Lorilleux. They will be vexed because I am leaving them, but one day I have to get married. You are going to say yes. Oh, nothing can prevent you from it.

GERVAISE

If I was sure— (at this moment Gouget enters and seeing Coupeau taps him on the shoulder)

COUPEAU (turning)

Heavens! Golden Throat.

GOUGET (after having greeted Gervaise)

Say, you haven't seen my men around here. Works pressing at the blacksmith's and everybody's acting as if it were a holiday.

COUPEAU (pointing to the Dram Shop)

I've seen Mes-Bottes. He went in there.

GOUGET

That's always where you have to look for them. (goes into the Dram Shop)

GERVAISE

Throat of Gold, that's yet another nickname, right?

COUPEAU

Yes, because of his beautiful yellow beard! His name's Gouget. A solid lad! And honest, and well organized! Who lives with his mother, a real woman, too, that one. You are going away?

GERVAISE (who has risen)

No question, I'm going. I've drunk my plum. (seeing Coupeau

drink the juice she left) What! You are finishing my glass?

COUPEAU

Now, it's done. I know what you are thinking.

GERVAISE

Oh! I really mean to tell you what I am thinking, My ideal would be to work quietly, to be sure of always having bread, a room, a bit nice—a bed, a table, two chairs, nothing more!

COUPEAU

Why, we'll have all that.

GERVAISE

There's still another ideal—that would be not to be beaten.

COUPEAU

Madame Gervaise, as for me, I will never beat you.

GERVAISE

Now that's all I want. In that case, life would be happy.

COUPEAU

Well! Say yes—and life will be happy.

(During the following, male and female workmen, employees pass by again. As Gouget speaks, they surround him, they end by forming a crowd.)

GOUGET (coming out of the Dram Shop and pushing Mes-Bottes in front of him)

Come on—head for the forge, work presses.

MES-BOTTES (rebellious)

Hey! Say, don't push I will go if I want to. (gesture by Gouget) Easy. People are around.

BEC-SALE (to Mes-Bottes)

What? You're leaving us?

BIBI

Don't you have more courage than that?

GOUGET (to Bibi and Bec-Sale)

The rest of you—shut up! Aren't you ashamed, a couple of good-for-nothings?

BIBI

Big words! What's he say, that guy?

GOUGET

I say, I say that you are loafers and no big deals, to spend your days, at a wine merchant's when work is waiting for you at the workyard. (to Mes-Bottes) As for you, I won't leave you.

BEC-SALE (ironic)

Ah! The gentleman takes on the interests of the bosses. The

gentleman is for the exploiters?

BIBI

Bosses are no longer needed. (the workers approach and form a circle around Gouget)

VARIOUS VOICES

No, no—no longer needed! Quite so!

A WOMAN OF THE PEOPLE (to a worker)

What's going on?

WORKER

That fellow's attacking the workers.

BEC-SALE (hopping in front of Gouget)

There's one who fattens on the sweat of the people.

BIBI

And we—are—the people!

SEVERAL VOICES

Yes, yes—we are!

GOUGET (with brilliance)

You, the people? You who rise in the morning still drowsy with the intoxication of the evening, who drag yourselves from counter to counter, leaving a bit of your reason in all the glasses, you lack the strength to hold a tool in your trembling hands, who at night fall into a corner to begin the same shameful life the next morning. You, the people? Come on!

BEC-SALE

Has he finished insulting everybody?

A WORKER

No, no, let him talk.

GOUGET

Hear me! It's the real people I defend. Are the real people the wretches who allow mothers and little ones to die in a garret? Are the real people the drunks who roll little by little towards the sewer, dirty, tattered, maddened by drink and misery? (pointing to the Dram Shop) See, your misfortune comes from there. One day you enter. A small glass and it's without consequence. Then Brandy takes you in the guts. The little glasses keep coming, and you end by drinking vitriol in large ones. Then, you are ruined. There's no longer a God, there's no more wife, no more kids, no more wash, no more nothing. You become brutes, worse than mad dogs! (movement by the workers) Come on, don't say you are the people. It's you who besmirch it—it's because of you they are misunderstood and distrusted. Close those poison factories. Stop drinking, wretches, and work. The people will be great.

ALL

Bravo! Bravo!

GERVAISE

Ah! The brave lad! You heard him, Mr. Coupeau. Never drink!

COUPEAU

There's no danger, I love you too much.

GERVAISE

Well, in that case.

COUPEAU

Well?

GERVAISE

I say—yes!

COUPEAU (hugging her)

Ah! Gervaise! My wife.

GERVAISE

And may God forgive us if we are doing something crazy.

GOUGET (to Mes-Bottes)

Come to the work shop. The rest of you—let us pass.

THE CROWD

Bravo, blacksmith. Bravo, Golden Throat. (applause by the crowd)

CURTAIN

ACT II
SCENE 4

The Silver Mill. A big garden of a restaurant. To the left and back. To the right the restaurant is seen at an angle.

AT RISE, Adolph is giving orders to waiters who place tables in arbors. Lantier is seated at a table on the right, reading a paper and drinking a glass of absinthe.

ADOLPH (to waiters)

Come on, come on, gang. Hurry up a little! This is the hour the customers will arrive. (to Lantier) Must we set your table in an arbor, sir?

LANTIER

Yes, in an arbor.

ADOLPH

Do you want dinner right away?

LANTIER

Right away.

ADOLPH (shouting)

A table set in an arbor. (to Lantier) At the back, sir.

LANTIER (in the restaurant)

Waiter! Waiter!

ADOLPH

Coming! Coming! (to waiters) Come on, gang, a little activity. (the waiters leave)

MADAME GOUGET (entering with Gouget, speaking to her son)

Now, where is it you're taking me, my child?

GOUGET

To The Silver Mill. The best restaurant in La Chapelle.

ADOLPH (pointing to an arbor at the left)

You do well to get here early. Number four is free.

MADAME GOUGET (to Adolph)

You're expecting a lot of company?

ADOLPH

Yes, today's Saturday. We've got two weddings. One is already installed in a room upstairs, and the other one won't be late. It can make your head spin. (to a waiter) Two settings at arbor 4, and be quick about it! (he leaves)

MADAME GOUGET

It would have been better for us to make dinner at home.

GOUGET

For which you are much too sick, right? I intend for you to rest today. It's been a rough week. We've worked hard every day. What the devil! It's really necessary to have a little pleasure.

MADAME GOUGET

We're so peaceful at home in our little household.

GOUGET

No, no. I said to myself, "It's a nice day, I'm going to escort Mama Gouget to a restaurant, and after dinner we will go to the theatre."

MADAME GOUGET

The way you are spoiling me!

GOUGET

Never as much as you spoiled me, dear mother.

MADAME GOUGET

How good you are! Ah, heaven has rewarded me in you for all I suffered before.

GOUGET (excitedly)

Never speak of that! I have strong arms, I earn enough to make savings which will permit me, perhaps, to become a boss in my turn. What more could we want?

MADAME GOUGET

As for me, I desire something: to find a wife worthy of you.

GOUGET: (smiling)

Still at your idea.

MADAME GOUGET

I will be so satisfied.

GOUGET

It will happen one day or another. No rush. Look, what do you want to eat: a pigeon with small peas, with lots of lard?

MADAME GOUGET

Oh, if you snare me through my weakness (laughing, they disappear into the arbors)

MES-BOTTES (entering with Bibi, both in Sunday best)

What—fucking heat!

ADOLPH

What do these gentlemen want?

MES-BOTTES

We are guests at the wedding of Mr. Coupeau.

ADOLPH

Ah, very fine. (starting to leave)

MES-BOTTES

When do we eat?

ADOLPH

At six, sir.

MES-BOTTES

Another half hour. Never have I waited so long. Serve me some bread and brie to amuse me.

BIBI

With two liters for each of us.

ADOLPH

Right way, gentlemen. (he leaves)

MES-BOTTES

Jesus! How thirsty it makes you!

BIBI

Need to wet our whistles, What.

MES-BOTTES

That is to say, just now, as I came in, I almost stopped before a fountain.

BIBI

Luckily, I was there. If someone had seen you. (Adolph brings two liters, cheese, and a serving of bread).

MES-BOTTES (looking at the bread)

Waiter. What's, this, waiter?

ADOLPH

It's bread.

MES-BOTTES

That's bread. Ah, indeed. Waiter. Do you take me for an Englishman? Get me a loaf, a whole loaf, you understand?

ADOLPH (leaving)

Fine, sir.

MES-BOTTES (sitting down)

That's telling him, that character!

BIBI (also sitting)

To your health, old boy.

MES-BOTTES

To yours. (drinking) It's not bad, this little blue—

BIBI

You don't detest the color, huh?

MES-BOTTES

That is to say, I'll end by believing at my birth, Mama dedicated me to blue—(the waiter brings an enormous loaf of bread)

BIBI

With a baguette like that, you've got something to stuff your rifle with.

BEC-SALE

(coming out of the restaurant) Waiter! You're not forgetting us up there?

ADOLPH

Right away, sir, right away.

MES-BOTTES

Heavens! Bec-Sale.

BEC-SALE

(with astonishment) Mes-Bottes. Bibi the Grillarde. Now there's a meeting.

BIBI

What are you doing here?

BEC-SALE

I'm at Poisson's wedding.

MES-BOTTES

Ah! This is really good! Then it's for this you borrowed— my trousers? The rest of us are here for Coupeau's wedding.

BEC-SALE

(laughing) Then it's complete. The two weddings the same day, the same place! Hush! Here's my bride! She doesn't know a thing. It's a big farce!

VIRGINIA

(enters dressed as a bride with a white bouquet) Well! Aren't they serving us?

BIBI

(stupefied) Ah! Swanky! (to Mes-Bottes) Take a gander at the orange flower.

MES-BOTTES

Have to think it's not expensive this year.

BEC-SALE

Say there, Madame Poisson, you're going to see a friend, Madame Gervaise.

VIRGINIA

(shaking) Ah!

BEC-SALE

She's marrying Coupeau! They're having the wedding here!

VIRGINIA

(completely thunderstruck) Here!

MES-BOTTES

(to Bec-Sale) It's funny how that pleases her.

BEC-SALE

(low) They are going to have a row. (to Virginia, pointing to his two comrades) These are two of Coupeau's guests that I am presenting to you.

VIRGINIA

(curtsying) Gentlemen.

BIBI

The rest of us, we've been on a lark.

BEC-SALE

As for us, we've been shut in upstairs since noon. We're playing cards.

VIRGINIA

That's because of the rain.

MES-BOTTES

As for us, we went to the museum.

VIRGINIA

The Museum! What's that?

MES-BOTTES

At the Tuilleries, or rather in a house next door. It's so touching.

VIRGINIA

You're joking.

MES-BOTTES

Not at all. There were twelve of us, and folks very chic. Mr. Madinier, the landlord, Mr. Lorilleax who manufactures gold chains, Madame Lorilleaux, Mrs. Remajou.

BIBI

The whole shebang—what!

MES-BOTTES

And did we see curiosities at the Louvre! Oh! First of all a floor! You could spread out in it. then pictures and more pictures. If only one had money for the frames. You've got to see it.

BEC-SALE

Jesus! If you'd told me in advance!

VIRGINIA

(disdainful) Leave off—scandals.

BEC-SALE (low to the other two)

She's raging because she doesn't have four cats at her wedding, and that pisses her off so she wants to swallow her tongue.

VIRGINIA (jesting)

And they stayed to dine at the Tuilleries, your comrades?

MES-BOTTES

No, they're in the Column. An idea that suddenly came to them to climb up to see Paris. We left them because the Column, is just not our style.

BIBI

Say, all the same, suppose we go to meet them?

MES-BOTTES

I'd really like that.

BEC-SALE

I'm going with you, I'll be back right away, Madame Poisson. (they leave)

VIRGINIA (alone)

So, I will forever meet this woman. (Lantier, who's emerged from an arbor is slowly approaching her and places his hand on her shoulder.) You! What did you come here for?

LANTIER

I just dined there.

VIRGINIA

Why, then, you don't know?

LANTIER

I know there are two weddings at the Silver Mill tonight. As for me, I am curious. It's quite all right to dine at a restaurant.

VIRGINIA

You came for Gervaise?

LANTIER

Now there's an idea for heaven's sake! because I no longer want her—

VIRGINIA

There are women you no longer want, but that you love again when you see them with another.

LANTIER:

You detest her so much?

VIRGINIA

Oh, yes, I detest her! Listen, Lantier, tell me you don't love her.

LANTIER

Because?

VIRGINIA (with fury)

Because I don't want you to love her!

LANTIER (smiling)

That's sweet! Don't worry—if Gervaise isn't reasonable, the two of us will work for her happiness.

VIRGINIA

You don't love her?

LANTIER

(jesting) Curious. Goodbye, my beauty.

VIRGINIA

You're leaving?

LANTIER

No. I'm taking a stroll. It's really permitted to take a stroll. Bye—and all my wishes for prosperity, my darling.

(he disappears)

VIRGINIA (alone)

He still loves her, I see that plain enough. Oh, that Gervaise! If we were to meet! What to do?

(she goes back into the restaurant)

BIBI (returning with his comrades)

They're still not here!

BEC-SALE

There's nothing to understand about it.

MES-BOTTES

Could they be locked in the Column?

(uproar outside)

BEC-SALE

There they are, no doubt. (Bazouge enters, mildly drunk, and turns towards the folks who hoot him.)

BAZOUGE

Bunch of imbeciles!

MES-BOTTES

Screw it! No! It's not the wedding.

BAZOUGE (to Adolph who enters)

Waiter. A giblet and a liter.

(he disappears)

MES-BOTTES (to Adolph)

Say there. You've got a funny customer, there.

ADOLPH

Ah, yes, Papa Bazouge. He's not bad. He's even a bon-vivant, despite his condition. (he leaves)

BEC-SALE (philosophically)

After all, everybody's got to live.

(uproar)

BIBI

This time. That's our wedding.

COUPEAU (entering with Gervaise)

That's not bad. Finally we got here.

LORILLEUX

You might say it was a tiring day, right, Madame Lorilleux?

MADAME LORILLEUX

Say, killing work, Mr. Lorilleux. I've ruined my silk dress.

MADAME BOCHE

God's Judgment! Well, I have something to tell Boche tonight on the pillow.

MADAME LORILLEUX

That Madame Boche. Always a nuisance!

GERVAISE

(to COUPEAU who kisses her) Stop! They're looking at us.

MADAME BOCHE

You think you're in the Column where it's so dark. They even pinched my waist.

MES-BOTTES (very gracious)

It was probably someone who made a mistake.

MADAME BOCHE

Fat rude man!

COUPEAU

Say! We must get some refreshments. (calling) Waiter!

ADOLPH (appearing)

I'm here.

COUPEAU

Bring us some beer.

MADAME BOCHE

And some liqueurs for the ladies.

(Adolph leaves)

MADAME LORILLEUX (continuing a conversation with Madinier)

No question, Mr. Madinier. The family, perhaps, would be desired. One always has plans. But things turn out so strange. As for me, first of all, I never like to argue.

LORILLEUX

So your brother would have brought up the last of the last, except I told him once again: Marry her and leave us alone!

MADINIER

And we were right a hundred times. In families it's necessary that each contribute his own.

(Adolph brings in beer and liqueurs)

COUPEAU

Come on, let's refresh ourselves. (to Gervaise) You will take a glass of liqueur with water.

GERVAISE

Yes—with a lot of water.

MADAME BOCHE (after having swallowed a drink)

Ah! That makes you feel good while it goes down.

MES-BOTTES

I need some of that.

MADAME LORILLEUX (to Gervaise)

Well? How do you feel?

GERVAISE

Fine, I thank you.

MADAME LORILLEUX

Because you have a strong appearance like that—Say, Mr. Lorilleux?

LORILLEUX

What is it, Madame Lorilleux?

MADAME LORILLEUX

Don't you think our sister-in-law resembles Therese—you know, that woman who lived opposite us and died suddenly of a heart ailment.

LORILLEUX

Indeed—there's a false appearance.

GERVAISE

My new relatives are amiable?

ADOLPH (entering, to Coupeau)

Pardon, sir. Should I put the consommé on the bill?

COUPEAU

No. How much?

ADOLPH

With two liters and your bread, six francs eight sou.

COUPEAU

There. Dinner's been ordered. A picnic at five francs a head.

ADOLPH

Yes, sir. Potage with pasta, veal stew with sorrel— Rabbit giblets. Shank. Salad. Dessert.

MES-BOTTES

Perfect! Very chic!

MADINIER

Very fine indeed, Except for the potage. I was hoping for it.

BEC-SALE (amazed)

What's this, a potage?

ADOLPH

It's made with veal.

COUPEAU (to ADOLPH)

Then we'd like some like that, It's understood. (to Madinier) You're satisfied, Mr. Madinier?

MADINIER

I'm far from disapproving the menu, but I will point out one more lacuna.

ADOLPH

A lacuna?

BEC-SALE

What's that?

BIBI

That it's made with veal.

MADINIER

I don't see depicted a sugared sweets for the ladies.

GERVAISE

That's true. What could they take?

MES-BOTTES

A salad of hard-boiled eggs.

MADAME BOCHE

That's not a sugared sweet—

MADINIER

I propose eggs a la niège.

BEC-SALE

Eggs à la niège. That's a chic dish, that is.

COUPEAU (to Adolph)

Then eggs à la niège, it's agreed, One doesn't get married every day.

MADAME LORILLEUX

(low to her husband) He's got it! There are some who do.

LORILLEUX (looking at Gervaise)

Yes, there are some who marry every day.

BEC SALE (to Mes-Bottes)

Yes, eggs à la niège. I've always wanted to eat that dish. For sure, there won't be any at Poisson's dinner.

MES-BOTTES

Leave Poisson's wedding.

BEC-SALE

I cannot. And the conventions.

MES-BOTTES

Never mind the conventions.

VIRGINIA (leaving the restaurant)

Well! Waiter, aren't you thinking of us at all?

GERVAISE (aside)

Virginia!

COUPEAU

What's wrong with you, Gervaise?

GERVAISE

Me? Nothing!

MES-BOTTES (low)

Attention! There's the squabble coming.

LORILLEUX

This is going to be funny. (Virginia slowly comes toward Gervaise who watches her come, terrified)

VIRGINIA

Huh? How we meet! We didn't expect to find each other here the day of our marriage.

GERVAISE (very moved)

Ah, you, too—you—?

POISSON (entering, to Virginia)

What's up?

VIRGINIA (to Poisson)

An old friend with whom we were a bit cold, But, we no longer have it in for each other, right?

(offering her hand to Gervaise)

GERVAISE (hesitating)

What—you want to?

VIRGINIA

I'm not mean and if it suits you, let's forget the past.

GERVAISE (shaking Virginia's hand)

With pleasure.

VIRGINIA

And we'll become friends, good friends!

GERVAISE

I ask nothing better.

MES-BOTTES (aside)

Beneath all this there's some trick.

VIRGINIA

I present my husband, Mr. Poisson.

GERVAISE

And me, mine, Mr. Coupeau.

POISSON (to Coupeau)

Delighted to make your acquaintance.

COUPEAU (to Poisson)

Equally delighted. (they shake hands, Mes-Bottes, Bibi, and Bec-Sale come to greet them. Poisson bows very stiffly)

BIBI (to Mes-Bottes)

He's not talkative, that fellow.

BEC-SALE

Oh, I've got an idea. I propose to join the two weddings together.

ALL

Yes, yes, accepted.

BEC-SALE (to Mes-Bottes)

This way I get to eat eggs à la niège.

COUPEAU (to Adolph who appears)

Could you serve the two dinners together?

ADOLPH

Nothing could be easier. I ask only a quarter of an hour to arrange the two settings upstairs.

COUPEAU

Very well. Hum. What are we going to do while waiting? (an orchestra can be heard) Heavens—there's dancing?

ADOLPH

Yes, sir, at the back of the garden.

COUPEAU

Wonderful! We are going to grab a quadrille to give you time to set the tables.

All

Yes, yes, a quadrille. (they leave in a hurry some already dancing.)

COUPEAU (to Gervaise)

Aren't you coming?

GERVAISE (seated)

I'll join you, my friend, I'm a bit exhausted and my head's spinning. Oh, don't worry.

COUPEAU

That's fine. I'll wait for you.

GERVAISE

(alone) I'm very sad—that Virginia reminds me of the past. But I want to be happy. I want to chase off my presentments. (At this moment, Lantier who's left an arbor—appears before her.)

LANTIER

Hello, Madame Coupeau.

GERVAISE (recoiling, very frightened)

Lantier!

LANTIER

Well, yes, me. Does it surprise you?

GERVAISE

What do you want? This isn't your place here?

LANTIER

Ah, you're not nice! I, who came to bring you my congratulations on the subject of your marriage.

GERVAISE

I really hoped never to see you again after the shameful manner in which you behaved towards me.

LANTIER

My God! I admit it. I did wrong. But why did you conclude this marriage so abruptly?

GERVAISE

I don't have to account to you. We no longer exist for each other.

LANTIER

Then don't say anything. I can still be your friend.

GERVAISE

Never!

LANTIER (with cajolery)

We will see. All isn't known to be finished between us. Do you hear? Gervaise, I want to see you again.

GERVAISE

Let me alone or I'll call.

LANTIER

Call. Who's that? Your husband? Well, at your ease, my sweet. Call. Have the whole wedding party. Call.

GERVAISE (terrified)

Shut up. For pity—

LANTIER

Come on, Don't be naughty, my dear. (he wants to take her in his arms)

GERVAISE

Go away, go away, I tell you! (Lantier tries to pull her to him, but Gervaise fights.)

GOUGET (entering and seeing Lantier pursuing Gervaise)

Will you leave this woman in peace!

LANTIER

Where's this one come from? Mind your own business!

GOUGET

It is my business. I will never let a coward insult a woman in front of me.

LANTIER

A coward!

GOUGET

Yes, a coward. Get going. Decamp! If not (he threatens him)

LANTIER

(showing lack of courage) If you think to scare me.

GOUGET

Ah, don't steam me up. Beat it, or I whack you—

LANTIER

That's good. I don't box like a porter (at a gesture from Gouget he heads towards the back, then in a threatening tone.) We will see each other again. (he leaves)

GOUGET

Don't be frightened any more. Take my arm, I beg you.

(he offers her his arm and they walk for a moment together)

GERVAISE

Ah, how I thank you, Mr. Gouget.

GOUGET (surprised)

What—you know my name?

GERVAISE

Yes. I saw you before—one morning when you went to find your men at the dram shop.

GOUGET (laughing)

That happens so often.

GERVAISE

You are good to have taken up my defense, someone you don't know! If you knew!

GOUGET

I don't wish to know.

GERVAISE

You must be careful—he's a bad man.

GOUGET (shrugging his shoulders)

Him? Come on! He's a capon! A man who insults women.

GERVAISE

Promise me that you will be on your guard.

GOUGET (smiling)

Ah, indeed! Why, you really are a good-hearted little thing.

GERVAISE

I love people who are good to me and who are brave.

GOUGET

I bet you're a very good and sweet little woman. What's your name?

GERVAISE

Gervaise. Coupeau.

GOUGET

Wait. I remember now, I saw you with him, You're his relative?

GERVAISE

From this morning, I am his wife.

GOUGET (releasing her arm)

His wife—Ah!

GERVAISE

What's the matter?

GOUGET

Nothing. (aside) His wife! (one hears the dancers returning, couple by couple.)

GERVAISE

Will you do me the pleasure of being present at our wedding?

GOUGET

Thanks. I am with my mother. All the same, I am pleased to have seen you again. And if one day I can be useful to you in some way—

GERVAISE

For my part—never. I will never forget you. Never!

GOUGET

Goodbye!

GERVAISE

Goodbye! Thanks. Thanks a lot!

GOUGET (aside, as he leaves)

His wife! That's a shame! (he disappears)

(The couples enter, dancing the quadrille and envelop the stage.)

COUPEAU (entering with Virginia)

Now there are some crazies! (to Gervaise) You didn't come?

GERVAISE

I told you I was tired.

ADOLPH (appearing in the doorway)

Ladies and Gentlemen—you will be served in five minutes. (the music resumes)

MADAME BOCHE

Come on, let's finish our quadrille.

MES-BOTTES

What boring person to get rid of—Madame Boche is (passing her to Bibi) All yours, Bibi.

BIBI

Thanks a lot—Bye! (he passes her to Bec-Sale)

BEC-SALE (receiving her)

With pleasure! I couldn't ask for more.

COUPEAU

Ah, my little wife. You're going to dance with me.

MES-BOTTES

No, not with you. (to Coupeau) You've got plenty of time, you do.

VIRGINIA

With me, Mr. Coupeau.

BEC-SALE

Two forward!

(Quadrille. Two steps by Mes-Bottes who dances with Madame Boche. At this moment Bazouge appears totally drunk. He starts staggering in the midst of the Quadrille. The women, noticing him, let out a scream of terror. The Quadrille stops.)

GERVAISE (uttering a scream)

Ah!

BAZOUGE

I frighten you; Stupidities, go way. I am as good as anyone else. (to Gervaise) Would you like to dance with Bibi, says the consoler of ladies.

GERVAISE (frightened)

Don't touch me. (at a gesture by Bouzage she screams) (to Coupeau, seeking refuge in his arms) Coupeau!

COUPEAU (to Bazouge)

Will you get out of here. (to Adolph) You shouldn't let people like this enter.

BAZOUGE (To Gervaise, shrugging his shoulders)

Nothing's preventing you from passing, my little one. You will be quite content to pass one day. Yes, I know women who would say thanks if they were carried off—!

GERVAISE (terrified)

Ah! (they press around her. Adolph and the waiters drag Bazouge off.)

CURTAIN

ACT III (1858)
SCENE 5

The House in repair. A work space encumbered with big cut stones. To the left, a house with a platform in front of it. A large scaffolding. A street passes in the back.

Bibi, Bec-Sale, and the stone masons are working on the scaffolding. Coupeau, below, is busy shaping some zinc on a work bench.

BIBI (to Bec-Sale)

Say, old boy—what time is it?

BEC-SALE

I don't know. Since last month my watch is slow a dozen francs.

BIBI

A dozen francs! It's then not on time?

BEC-SALE

I really think so. It's that wise guy of a Lantier who sold it to me at twenty sous a week.

BIBI

On the subject of Lantier, what's become of him that oddball?

BEC-SALE

I heard it said that he left for England to put up a—beaver hat factory.

BIBI (to a worker beneath him)

Hey! L'Ecuriel—send me a bucket of water.

(the worker hooks a pail to a rope, Bibi hoists it up. The pail reaches the first level and breaks a pane of glass.)

COUPEAU

(singing) One more pane broken. There's the glass man passing by.

BIBI

Ah, dammit. I did a fine thing. Right in Madame Poisson's window.

VIRGINIA

(opening the window) Well, that's nice. Who is it broke me a pane?

BEC-SALE (laughing)

Pay no attention, Madame Poisson, it's to keep business going.

VIRGINIA

The dust is going to come into my home so beautifully. What an idea the landlord had to add a floor to his house.

BEC-SALE

Hell—where are the tenants?

BIBI

Don't worry yourself. We'll soon be finished.(shouting to Coupeau) Right Coupeau?

COUPEAU

(raising his head) Huh? What's up? (noticing Virginia) Hello, Madame Poisson! How's your husband?

VIRGINIA

Not bad. Still trying to obtain a position as a police man.

BIBI

It seems difficult to get into the station house.

BEC-SALE

There are some who pretend it's even harder to get out.

VIRGINIA (shutting the window)

Ah, the damned dust. (she disappears)

MES-BOTTES (entering, to Coupeau)

Hello, old boy.

COUPEAU

What have you come here for?

MES-BOTTES

I'm bringing some beams for this building. Still happy?

COUPEAU

Yes, indeed, thanks.

MES-BOTTES

Family's well?

COUPEAU

Very well! Gervaise, my little Nana—Everybody's going like a charm!

MES-BOTTES

Ah, as for you, you're happy!

COUPEAU

The fact is, I'd be wrong to complain. For the seven years I've been married, everything I've done succeeds.

MES-BOTTES

You've got luck! And all this, because you don't have a hole under your nose that's thirsty like I do.

BIBI (noticing Mes-Bottes)

Hey! Mes-Bottes!

MES-BOTTES

(looking in the air) Bibi and Bec-Sale! What are you doing up there?

BEC-SALE

(proudly) We're working.

MES-BOTTES: You are working! Now there are some loafers.

(eleven o'clock strikes.)

BEC-SALE

Eleven o'clock. Soup time!

BIBI

Come on down, fast.

(they come down as the other workers are leaving)

MES-BOTTES (laughing)

Huh! Don't get dragged off.

BEC-SALE

Are you coming to lunch with us?

MES-BOTTES

I have to put my beams up there. (he goes up the scaffolding)

BIBI

Hurry up. We're waiting for you.

BEC-SALE (to Coupeau)

And you, you're not coming?

COUPEAU

Thanks. The Boss-lady has to bring me a mouthful.

BEC-SALE

More than that sort—

COUPEAU

And while waiting, I'm going to find Zedoro, my poltroon of an apprentice who left twenty minutes ago to get some zinc. I bet he's playing—horseshoes—on the square. (leaves)

BEC-SALE (to Mes-Bottes who's on the scaffolding)

Well, how is it?

MES-BOTTES

A moment! Ah, indeed, friends, your scaffolding is unstable—! There's a plank that's wobbling—

BIBI

Yes, we'll fix it after lunch. Come on, come down.

MES-BOTTES (coming back down)

That would make a famous fall down all the same. The comrades are informed?

BIBI

Certainly. Ah, why, no! and Coupeau. They didn't tell Coupeau a thing?

MES-BOTTES

Screw it! Got to warn him. Where is he?

BIBI

He left in search of his apprentice.

MES-BOTTES

What to do? (seeing Virginia leave the house) Ah, Mrs. Poisson. Are you absenting yourself for a long while?

VIRGINIA

I'm not going out. I'm coming down to work there in the shade, in the work area.

MES-BOTTES

Then when Coupeau returns tell him not to go up on the scaffolding.

VIRGINIA

For goodness sakes, why?

BIBI

Because it's not secure.

VIRGINIA

Ah, my God.

MES-BOTTES

Coupeau would risk breaking his neck.

VIRGINIA:

Don't worry, I'm here.

BIBI

Are you coming?

MES-BOTTES

Here I am. (to Virginia) I'm counting on you.

VIRGINIA

Yes, yes, have no fear. The time to go borrow, a chair from the concierge and I'm installed. (the workers and Virginia leave. At this moment Coupeau enters from the opposite direction with Zedoro.)

COUPEAU (holding Zedoro by the ear)

Ah, little wise-guy.

ZEDORO

Oh, there, there. Don't pull too hard, boss, they're long enough already..

COUPEAU

That will teach you to play at horseshoes when there's work to do. And now, go put the irons in the fire on the roof.

ZEDORO

Yes, boss. (aside) Old ape! (going up the ladder.)

COUPEAU

Well, where are you going?

ZEDORO

On the roof.

COUPEAU

You want to use the ladder.

ZEDORO

Why, boss, indeed, you go up that way.

COUPEAU (making him come down)

Those machines are not made for kids like you. Come on, decamp!

ZEDORO

Yes, boss. (he disappears into the house)

COUPEAU (alone, resuming his work)

I'm going to finish cutting the zinc. All the same, I'm beginning to get hungry.

(Zedoro emerges on the roof. Gervaise and Nana enter each carrying a mess tin)

NANA

Papa! Papa! Here's your lunch!

COUPEAU

Ah, finally. (kissing Nana) Hello, little girl.

NANA

Hello, little Papa.

GERVAISE

We are a little late.

COUPEAU

I'll eat better for it, because I've got an appetite.

GERVAISE (looking around)

Where do you want to eat?

COUPEAU (pointing to a stone)

There. (and he goes to wash his hands in water.)

NANA

I'm going to help you, Mama. (Nana and Gervaise place the mess tins on a big stone which they cover with a place setting)

ZEDORO (appearing on the roof)

Well, boss, aren't you coming up?

COUPEAU

Heat the irons while I'm having lunch. (to Gervaise) What's that you've brought me there?

GERVAISE

A nice soup and lamb stew.

NANA

With some salad. I was the one who tossed it.

COUPEAU

(laughing) Ah, bah!

NANA

Oh, I am very strong, I am, to toss the salad. Right, Mama?

GERVAISE

A real little woman.

COUPEAU (to Gervaise who serves him the soup)

What a perfume it exudes. (to Nana) What about you? Have you had lunch?

NANA

Yes, Papa. I lunched with Mama.

GERVAISE

Miss doesn't want to eat the soup.

COUPEAU

No soup! Why that's very ugly. Little girls who don't eat soup will never grow big.

NANA

Oh, you think so?

COUPEAU

Certainly. (he takes her and sits her on his knees)

NANA

Dada! Dada! Papa's a horse!

GERVAISE

Let your father eat in peace.

NANA

I want him to be a horse.

COUPEAU (laughing and making Nana jump)

When Miss gets on her horse, it goes clop, clop, trot, trot, then gallops—there!

NANA

Again!

GERVAISE (to Coupeau)

Put her on the ground. She's in your way.

NANA

In that case, give me your soup.

COUPEAU

What! You want soup now?

NANA

Because you said it makes me grow.

COUPEAU (giving her a ladle of soup)

Is it good?

NANA

Oh, yes, Papa.

GERVAISE (to Nana)

Then why didn't you eat it at home?

NANA

Because it tastes better in Papa's mess tin.

COUPEAU (to Gervaise)

Pass me the ragout.

NANA (getting off his knees)

I'm going to play. Hey, do you want to, Papa?

COUPEAU

Go ahead, but be careful not to touch my tools. (Nana sits on the ground and plays with pieces of zinc.) Why did you come so late?

GERVAISE (smiling)

I am a little amazed. I don't dare tell you.

COUPEAU

What is it then?

(Virginia appears and eavesdrops)

GERVAISE

Well. The little Milliner's shop you know Rue Goutte d'Or?

COUPEAU:

I know—in Lorilleux's house.

GERVAISE

It's for rent.

COUPEAU

Ah.

GERVAISE

That would suit me perfectly—to establish myself as a laundress

COUPEAU (smiling)

Ambitious woman, go away!

GERVAISE

Only, it's very expensive. The landlord is talking 500 francs per year.

COUPEAU

Then you asked the price?

GERVAISE

Oh, you know, from curiosity. That doesn't commit to anything. But, no—decidedly, it's too expensive.

COUPEAU (smiling)

The fact is that 500 francs—you really would like to have it?

GERVAISE

Oh, like is not the word. Besides, perhaps we can obtain a reduction.

COUPEAU

Come on, admit that you want it.

GERVAISE (without answering)

Madame Gouget, who I consulted, very much approves of my idea of establishing myself.

COUPEAU

Ah, Madame Gouget approves.

GERVAISE

Yes, we've got money. Our savings which are at the Savings Bank.

COUPEAU

Well, in that case, don't hesitate.

GERVAISE

Really! You consent! How good you are! I am right to say it; now if you hadn't wanted it, I would have fallen ill from it. Ah, I love you. (she leaps on his neck. Nana finds them. They take her and kiss her, too.) Heavens! Look at the jealous thing.

VIRGINIA (appearing)

Well! Don't disturb yourselves!

GERVAISE

Oh, if you knew, Madame Poisson. Coupeau consents to me renting the shop in the Rue de la Goutte d'Or. I'm going to set myself up as a laundress.

VIRGINIA

My compliments.

COUPEAU

I hope that you will give your business to my wife?

VIRGINIA

What do you think! With pleasure.

ZEDORO (from the roof)

Boss, the irons are hot.

COUPEAU

To work.

GERVAISE (to Coupeau, removing the setting, helped by Nana)

After your day, come take me to Madame Fauconner's and we'll pass by the Rue de la Goutte d'Or.

COUPEAU

That's agreed. Bye for now.

GERVAISE

You've made me very happy! Do you see, because, perhaps, it's a fortune.

VIRGINIA

Yes, yes. She's going to be happy!

NANA

Kiss me, Papa!

COUPEAU (gaily, after having kissed her)

Come on, get going. I have to go up. (heads towards ladder.)

VIRGINIA (seeing him climb)

Mr. Coupeau!

COUPEAU (stopping)

What? Madame Poisson—

VIRGINIA (after hesitating)

Nothing. (she quickly goes back in to her house,)

GERVAISE (to Coupeau who's climbing the ladder)

Especially no carelessness! If you knew how much I tremble when I know you're between heaven and earth, in places where the larks themselves wouldn't risk themselves.

COUPEAU

There's no danger here. I'm going to work from the scaffold. It's as if I were on solid ground. (he climbs up, Gervaise turns her back busy taking the mess tins.)

GERVAISE (to Nana)

Nana, we're going home right away.

NANA

Yes, Mama. (turning) Bye, Papa. (blows him a kiss)

COUPEAU (at the top of the scaffolding)

Goodbye, daughter!

NANA

No, no—I can't see you completely. Bye, Papa. (she sends him more kisses)

COUPEAU (going toward the end of the plank)

Goodbye.

NANA

Come even closer, Like that: a kiss, two kisses.

COUPEAU (laughing, imitating her)

A kiss, two kisses.

NANA

Three kisses.

COUPEAU (repeating)

Three kisses. (the plank wobbles, he falls into the void)

GERVAISE (with a terrible scream)

Ah!

NANA

Papa!

GERVAISE

Help! Help! Ah, my God! What a misfortune. Coupeau, my poor Coupeau.

MES-BOTTES

He fell!

BIBI

Is he dead?

BEC-SALE

Possibly indeed.

BIBI

Go to him.

BEC-SALE

Ah! This ladder!

MES-BOTTES (aside)

Virginia didn't warn him.

BEC-SALE

Let's carry him to Lariboisene.

GERVAISE

To hospital? No, I don't want that. To our home, to our home.

(They carry Coupeau away using the ladder as a stretcher.)

CURTAIN

ACT III
SCENE 6

Gervaise's Party. A washerwoman's shop. A street door. A door giving on a kitchen. A laundress's furnace. A large laundry table that occupies most of the stage.

Clemence and Madame Putois are busy putting the setting on the work table.

MADAME PUTOIS

There, everything will soon be ready for the blow-out that Madame Coupeau is giving on the occasion of her party.

CLEMENCE

The small plates on the big as the saying goes.

MADAME PUTOIS (pointing to a board)

Place the flower pots we've offered to the Boss on that board. They are embarrassing.

CLEMENCE

All the same, it's nice of her to have invited us for dinner.

MADAME PUTOIS

Hell! That's very fair of her since we are going to eat at the work table.

CLEMENCE (laughing)

I think we ought to give more fork blows then are given iron blows.

AUGUSTINE (entering with an empty basket)

I've just taken linen to the customers. Jesus! What a setting!

CLEMENCE

You took your time, kid.

AUGUSTINE

I'm going to tell you what kept me. It's because I stopped at the Wine Seller on the corner to look at Mr. Coupeau.

CLEMENCE

The boss.

AUGUSTINE

Yes, he was drinking with his friends. Ah, they were not funny.

MADAME PUTOIS

Because he's returning to agreeable conditions. Yesterday, he was so gay!

CLEMENCE

It seems he wasn't drinking then.

AUGUSTINE

It's since his accident that he's taken to it. During his convalescence he began to frequent the Wine Seller.

MADAME PUTOIS

One glass leads to another. Ah, men!

AUGUSTINE

They're not big things.

GERVAISE (coming from the kitchen apron-pushed back)

Children. And the setting—how's it coming?

CLEMENCE

Look, Madame, this has never been seen in the Rue de la Goutte d'Or.

MADAME BOCHE (entering from the street)

I'm here! I've come to see what you're up to? Well? This famous goose?

MADAME PUTOIS

On the spit.

MADAME BOCHE

Ah, my darling. This is all they are talking about in the quarter.

GERVAISE (to workers)

Go watch it.

MADAME PUTOIS and CLEMENCE

Yes, Madame.

MADAME BOCHE

And pay careful attention. Not too close to the fire so it won't burn. Water it well! (Clemence and Madame Putois go into the kitchen)

MADAME BOCHE

Huh? Are you in one of your moods?

GERVAISE

Hell. This is the moment to shoot.

MADAME BOCHE

It's a long time from today to that terrible day. Six months ago.

GERVAISE

Yes, the accident that happened to my poor husband.

MADAME BOCHE

Ah, you spent some villainous moments.

GERVAISE

Luckily, we had some savings. Coupeau didn't lack a thing. Then when the cupboard was empty we found some good hearts.

MADAME BOCHE

Your neighbors, Mr. Gouget and his mother.

GERVAISE

Mr. Gouget behaved like a brother to us. And later, it's thanks to him that I was able to establish myself here. This shop. It was my dream.

MADAME BOCHE

In the end, you're happy.

GERVAISE

Yes, indeed, happy. Very Happy.

MADAME BOCHE

You don't say that very gaily.

GERVAISE

There's no such thing as perfect joy.

MADAME BOCHE

Your marriage is on the rocks.

GERVAISE

I don't pity myself about that. No question: before he swore to me never to drink. Still, he's not bad to me—up till now.

MADAME BOCHE

You're afraid for later. Once the brandy seizes the man.

GERVAISE

Ah, heavens, let's not speak of that today To have peace in her household a woman must put up with a little—

MADAME BOCHE (aside)

I think it's not the moment to speak to her of that good-for-nothing Lantier that I saw prowling in the neighborhood. I must leave her in peace. (aloud) Say—how many will be here?

GERVAISE

There will be a dozen.

MADAME BOCHE

Well, if you like, there'll be fourteen.

GERVAISE

How's that?

MADAME BOCHE

Such as you see me, Madame Gervaise, I am charged as an ambassador. Yes, on the part of the Lorilleux, with whom you quarreled two months ago.

GERVAISE

Ah, the Lorilleux!

MADAME BOCHE

They ask to be reconciled with you.

GERVAISE

They were really bad during Coupeau's illness.

MADAME BOCHE

Look—on the occasion of your party.

GERVAISE

Indeed, I know one cannot remain quarreling in families!

MADAME BOCHE

And besides, they'll croak of jealousy seeing your dinner.

GERVAIS (laughing)

That decides me. Bring them, Madame Boche. Here', go through the kitchen you'll get home quicker. At seven, exactly, right? (Madame Boche leaves, Gervaise turns back toward the table.) Oh, those Lorilleux! Misers who lock themselves in when they have a good bit to eat for fear of being obliged to offer it to anyone, Let's see, we're going to need two more place settings. (she arranges the table)

GOUGET (entering with a superb floral display)

It is I, Madame Gervaise; I'm not disturbing you?

GERVAISE

Mr. Gouget. Ah, you are the first .

GOUGET

That's because we cannot come to dine tonight, So, I wanted to bring you—

GERVAISE

What! You cannot come to dinner? That's impossible! Your mother promised me.

GOUGET

You must excuse us, mother is a little ill.

GERVAISE

(uneasily) Ill?

GOUGET

Nothing worrisome, I assure you.

GERVAISE

By God! How much pain that causes me! Now there's all my pleasure ruined.

GOUGET (hesitating)

So, I wanted to bring you, if this doesn't annoy you—

GERVAISE

(smiling) No, no. This doesn't annoy me.

GOUGET

I wish you a nice party, Madame Gervaise. (He gives her the flowers.)

GERVAISE (smiling)

Well, is that all?

GOUGET (repeating)

A nice party. (she offers her cheek, he hesitates, but ends by kissing her. Both are shocked and embarrassed.)

(A silence)

GERVAISE (getting control of herself)

Your rose bush is superb. I'm going to put it there on the table in the place of honor. How vexed I am that you cannot come, you to whom I owe everything.

GOUGET

Don't mention it.

GERVAISE

Yes, yes. It was you who forced me to accept the 500 francs with which I was able to set myself up. And the money, your mother told me all about it, that money was destined for your marriage. I often repent not having refused.

GOUGET

There's nothing for you to repent. Go on! Yes, for a moment my mother would have wished—But I am the one who no longer wished.

GERVAISE

You no longer want to get married? Why's that?

GOUGET

Because I wouldn't be able to.

GERVAISE

You wouldn't be able to?

GOUGET

No, I've got another idea in mind.

GERVAISE

Ah. (a moment of embarrassment)

GOUGET

Yes, another idea. And the person isn't free.

GERVAISE (very upset)

I don't want to know your secrets. All that I know is that you've been indeed good, and that I will be eternally grateful to you.

GOUGET

Madame Gervaise—

GERVAISE

Oh, really, you can't prevent me from doing that.

GOUGET

Enough, I beg you. (he approaches her as if he wanted to take her in his arms, but recoils when Nana enters.)

NANA

Hello, Mama. I've come from school. Heavens! Mr. Gouget. Hello, Mr. Gouget.

GOUGET

Hello, my dear little Nana. (he kisses her feverishly on the face)

NANA

Oh, how hard you kissed me. You've never kissed me that hard.

GOUGET (very moved)

Goodbye, Madame Gervaise. (he leaves)

NANA

Mama, I'm bringing a compliment for you. Would you like me to read it to you?

GERVAISE (troubled)

Soon, before the company,

NANA

Give me ten sous to buy a red ribbon to put in my hair.

GERVAISE

(fumbling in her pocket) Here!

NANA

Thanks, Mama. I'm going to buy it right away. I want to be beautiful for the party. (she leaves. Hardly has she gone when Gervaise picks a rose from Gouget's rose bush and puts it in her corsage, without saying a word. Augustine, Madame Putois and Clemence appear in the kitchen door. At the same time Madame Boche and the Lorilleux enter from the street door.)

MADAME BOCHE (entering with a pot of flowers)

Ah, I hope I'm not the last. Let me wish you— (hugs her and gives her a bouquet.)

GERVAISE

Thanks, Madame Boche.

MADAME BOCHE

Here are your relatives.

GERVAISE

Come in, why, come right in.

MADAME BOCHE

What? They haven't even brought a bouquet of violets.

GERVAISE (embracing Madame Lorilleux)

It's over, right? We must become nice—the two of us.

MADAME LORILLEUX (very awkward)

I ask nothing better than for this to last forever.

LORILLEUX

You see, we've accepted your invitation. Where is Coupeau?

GERVAISE

He's going to come. Sit down, will you. I ask your pardon. I'm afraid the goose is burning.—Just a glance. (she hurries into the kitchen.)

MADAME LORILLEUX

Make yourself at home. (to her husband) What a setting!

LORILLEUX

Has she invited the whole neighborhood?

MADAME LORILLEUX

Where'd she get all that money?

LORILLEUX

Let's not investigate.

(Poisson appears with two pots of flowers)

POISSON

Where is Madame Coupeau?

MADAME BOCHE

She's in the kitchen. I'm going to tell her.—Madame Coupeau! Madame Coupeau!

GERVAISE (a ladle in hand)

I'm here. I'm here.

POISSON (offering her one of the pots)

Allow me to wish you a happy party. (he kisses her)

GERVAISE:

Thanks! Oh, beautiful flowers!

POISSON

You're Queen of them.

GERVAISE

Mr. Poisson, you are so gallant!

POISSON (presenting the other pot)

And now, here's the gift from my wife. She's coming behind me.

VIRGINIA (entering breathless)

It's me. At least I'm not late. (embracing Gervaise with affected effusion) All the prosperity, dear friend. (low) I have a word to tell you.

GERVAISE

To me?

VIRGINIA (pulling her into a corner)

Yes. (the others are moving chairs)

GERVAISE

What is it?

VIRGINIA

You mustn't be frightened. A person, a person that you know well has returned to Paris.

GERVAISE (shivering)

Lantier! You mean to speak of Lantier.

VIRGINIA

I was hesitating to talk to you about this, but I just saw him at the end of the street. I thought it was better to warn you.

GERVAISE

Ah, my God!

VIRGINIA

It's to be believed that he won't dare to show up here.

GERVAISE (terrified)

Coupeau would kill him.

LORILLEUX

Aren't we going to eat soon?

GERVAISE

In a minute, we're only waiting for the boss.

MADAME LORILLEUX

That way the soup has time to cool.

CLEMENCE (at the doorway to the street)

Here he is!

(Mes-Bottes, Bibi, and Bec-Sale enter with ridiculous flowers.)

COUPEAU (to his friends)

Come on, the rest of you, get here.

CLEMENCE (low to Gervaise)

Don't torture yourself, Madame. He's only a little bit lit up, but it can't be seen.

GERVAISE (reassured)

Yes, I was afraid.

MES-BOTTES (offering flowers)

On this day, accept this present with an open heart.

BEC-SALE (also offering flowers)

As for me, I won't say more, but I'm doing as much.

GERVAISE

Thanks, thanks.

COUPEAU (presenting a pot which he's hidden behind his back)

And me, Boss? Huh? I'm sweet. I think of my little woman. (kissing her) Heavens, my brother-in-law.

MES-BOTTES (pointing to Madame Lorilleux)

And your sister.

MADAME LORILLEUX

We've made peace with your wife.

COUPEAU

Right!

GERVAISE

Sit down!

MES-BOTTES

Hand to the ladies.

BIBI (low to Mes-Bottes)

Aren't you giving your hand to the beautiful Madame Poisson? She's so chic today!

MES-BOTTES (low)

No, I don't like that individual. She has eyes! Anyway, shush! I have my notion. (aloud) Let's go. Hand to the ladies.

(At the moment everyone sits down Nana enters with a ribbon in her hair and her compliment in her hand.)

NANA

And what about me?

GERVAISE

Sit beside Madame Poisson. And don't make any disturbance.

NANA

I'll have some of everything, right?

GERVAISE

Yes! Keep calm.

NANA

Is it time to read my compliment?

GERVAISE

Soon. After the potage.

AUGUSTINE

(bringing the potage) Here's the soup.

ALL

Ah!

COUPEAU

One moment! Before beginning, I propose to drink to the good health of the family.

(they drink and set about eating)

MES-BOTTES

Where's the bread?

MADAME BOCHE

Wait until you've finished your soup.

BIBI

Ah, well—you didn't know it. Now there's one who hides it.

In hiding.

BEC-SALE

It's not successful, this soup!

MES-BOTTES

Hum! A velvety taste—what.

MADAME BOCHE (to Mes-Bottes)

Don't eat your napkin, there'll be more.

NANA (to Gervaise)

Is it okay, now, to tell me?

GERVAISE

Yes, if you want to.

ALL

What is it?

GERVAISE

A compliment that Nana wrote—in boarding school—

ALL

The compliment! The compliment!

NANA (reading)

"Last night, my little guardian angel said to me: 'Tomorrow's your mother's birthday. You must make her a compliment, promise her always to be good, to always follow the path of duty and virtue so as to earn a place in paradise.'"

ALL

Bravo! Bravo!

GERVAISE (kissing her)

Darling little thing!

COUPEAU (moved)

The kid softened me up! It's stupid to weep like this. Let's drink to Nana's health.

ALL

To Nana's health.

NANA (to her father)

In addition, you'll give me ten sous, won't you, my dear little Daddy?

COUPEAU

Heavens: here's twenty.

MES-BOTTES

It's beginning to get hot in here. I ask the ladies for permission to take off my coat.

LADIES

Granted. Granted.

BIBI

In that case, I'm going to do like you. (Bibi and Bec-Sale remove their coats.)

COUPEAU

Indeed! We can even open the door!

VIRGINIA

Yes, that's it, open the door.

MADAME LORILLEUX

And the neighbors?

COUPEAU

I don't care a rap about the neighbors. We are at home, and if they are unhappy about it, they will come tell us.

AUGUSTINE (entering with a goose on a platter)

Here's the beast!

ALL

Bravo. (they beat the ground)

GERVAISE

Huh? You don't see one like that every day.

LORILLEUX (low to his wife)

That must have cost fifteen francs!

MADAME LORILLEUX

If it's not a shame to throw money out the window that way!

GERVAISE

Who's going to cut it?

CLEMENCE

That right reverts to Mr. Poisson who knows how to wield

weapons.

ALL

Yes, to Mr. Poisson.

POISSON

I am going to do my best to be worthy of your confidence. (he takes a knife, wipes it on his napkin and carves the goose.)

BEC-SALE

I propose to dig in!

ALL

That's it. Let's dig in.

GERVAISE (to Poisson)

Well, is it tender?

POISSON

Like a chicken! I am going to give you the Bishop's bonnet.

MADAME BOCHE

Only former soldiers know how to be agreeable in company.

POISSON

I will serve the ladies. (to Madame Lorilleux) What piece do you want?

MADAME LORILLEUX

I'll content myself with a wing, and a bit of white meat served with a slice of rump—

POISSON

There you are, Madame.

CLEMENCE

As for me, I'd like the skin.

MES-BOTTES

The skin is the slice for the ladies.

POISSON

And now let it circulate.

COUPEAU

Especially, let's water it. Let's water it.

CLEMENCE (low to her neighbor)

The boss is beginning to have a nice buzz on

POISSON

To the health of the Boss Lady. (at this moment, Lantier can be seen at the shop door.)

ALL

To the health of the Boss-Lady.

MADAME LORILLEUX (to Gervaise)

Who's that gentleman who's been lurking for the last few minutes. See there.

GERVAISE

Lantier!

COUPEAU

What's wrong with you? Why are you looking outside?

GERVAISE (trembling)

I'm not looking.

COUPEAU (seeing Lantier)

Him! That bastard! If you come in, I'll fix you.

LANTIER (in the doorway)

What's this? You're not allowed to pass in the street. They insult you!

COUPEAU (taking the carving knife to rush at him)

If you take a step, you won't leave here alive.

POISSON (disarming him)

No stupidities. (several guests rise to intervene.)

GERVAISE

Oh, my God!

LANTIER (taking a step into the shop)

If old friends refuse to recognize me, that's fine.

COUPEAU (furious)

Beat it or I'll strangle you.

VIRGINIA (who's come close to Lantier)

You came too soon. He hasn't drunk enough.

LANTIER

That's fine! That's fine! I am not seeking a quarrel with anyone. Let me leave peacefully. (he leaves)

(They all sit down again.)

MES-BOTTES (aside)

That brought on the cold.

AUGUSTINE (coming from the kitchen)

Here's the dessert.

MES-BOTTES

Oh, the dessert. That's for the ladies. If it's permitted, I prefer to toast one.

CLEMENCE

As you please.

BEC-SALE

Heavens! My old friend. Wouldn't this be the moment or each one to sing his song?

COUPEAU

I'd like that very well. Each one his song. And let's drink. (he pours cup after cup and drinks with a somber air)

MADAME BOCHE

Say, in that case, I will sing you: "Little kid, always stay small."

ALL

Yes, yes.

MADAME BOCHE (rising and singing)

Little child I've loved so tenderly
When I see you having fun.
And wildly running around the place.
Unable to catch the butterfly you're chasing
The storm's coming; lightning is breaking the clouds—
Come home fast child, here comes the night.
Your age alone knows gaiety

Little kid, stay small.

(Everyone applauds)

COUPEAU (drinking)

The second couplet?

ALL

Yes, yes, the second couplet.

MADAME BOCHE

I only know the first. If you like I'll start over.

BEC SALE

Ah, no.

MES-BOTTES

Well as for me. I know it. (sings)
Every morning when I rise
My heart feels topsy-turvy
I send it looking on the shore—
For a fish at four penny.

POISSON (furious)

A fish at four penny!

BIBI

Why, no. It's not about you.

POISSON

Ah, good.

MES-BOTTES

A fish at four penny
Three hours remain en route
And then in climbing up
I spill—half my dram
That rascally kid

(refrain)

(Everyone takes up the refrain.)

GERVAISE

My friend, don't drink any more. You're going to make yourself ill.

COUPEAU

You leave me alone, I'm thirsty.

MADAME LORILLEUX (low to Lorilleux)

Really, I no longer regret coming. It's funny.

NANA (starting to scream)

Oh. Oho. There Ouch!

GERVAISE

What's the matter with you, my dear?

NANA

I've got a booboo.

CLEMENCE

Poor little thing, she cut herself.

GERVAISE

Come, my dear. It won't be anything. (Nana and the women leave.)

POISSON

While, we're waiting for the coffee, we could all take air in the courtyard.

BIBI

That's a great idea. (they leave)

(Coupeau falls dead drunk on the table)

GERVAISE (wanting to take Coupeau)

Oh, the unfortunate. Coupeau, are you coming? (shaking him) Will you answer me, then! To put yourself in such a condition in front of everybody.

(seeing Lantier enter and letting out a scream) You again!

LANTIER

Yes, I expected you would be done.

GERVAISE (calling)

Coupeau! Coupeau!!

LANTIER

Listen, Gervaise, it's impossible that you've completely forgotten the past, that you don't remember what we were to one another. Remember down there in Plassons, how we loved each other? The first to who you said, "I love you"—it was me. You know it very well. And I want you to say it to me again. Yes, I've come to take you back; because you belong to me, yes to me.

GERVAISE (to Coupeau)

Coupeau—do you understand?

LANTIER

Eh, no, he doesn't understand. He's drunk. You can call him. He won't come to your aid.

GERVAISE (begging)

Coupeau, in the name of heaven, wake up!

COUPEAU (letting out a drunken sigh)

Hmmm!

LANTIER

Why do you refuse to follow me? What keeps you with this drunk?

GERVAISE

Leave me alone! (Lantier wants to take her in his arms and kiss her) No—no! (making a last effort) Coupeau! Protect me!

COUPEAU (finally raising his head)

Huh? What's the matter?

GERVAISE

See—He's come back!

COUPEAU (to Lantier)

Heavens! It's Lantier. Hello, my old friend.

GERVAISE

Why, didn't you hear! He wants to take me back. He wants to take me away with him.

COUPEAU

Ha! What a joker she is! (falls back on the table)

LANTIER

Well—you see?

GERVAISE (crazed)

My God! My God! I no longer have a husband. Wine's taken my husband. What am I going to do? Still, it's not my fault.

LANTIER (trying to drag her towards the door)

Follow me.

GERVAISE

Don't touch me! Never! Never!

(All the guests appear in the doorway, except Nana)

ALL

What's happening?

GERVAISE

Nothing. I don't need anyone. I know how to make myself respected. It's this man who introduced himself here that I am chasing out. Go on—Leave! Will you go, wretch!

LANTIER (low to Gervaise as he moves away)

You will pay me for this, little one. (he leaves)

VIRGINIA (aside)

I think that now he'll help me to avenge myself.

MES-BOTTES (laughing as he watches Lantier leave)

No luck today for the ladies hat maker.

CURTAIN

ACT IV (1860)
SCENE 7

The Dram Shop. A huge array of liqueurs. Tin countertop, big cases circled with shelves with crystal colored bottles. At the back the apparatus of a distillery is visible. A door on the side gives on a neighboring room. On the other side a door leading to the street decorated with glasses without—tin foil. Marble tables, chairs. The gas is lit.

AT RISE, Lantier is seated near the counter reading a paper while Bibi and Bec-Sale are seated at a table playing cards. Old Man Colombe pours rounds for the workers standing at the counter, Customers occupy several tables. Bazouge, at the back, silently drinks a glass of cognac.

BEC-SALE (to Bibi)

Your deal, my old buddy. (Bibi deals the cards.)

A Little Girl (entering)

Papa Colombe.

PAPA COLOMBE

What do you want, kid?

LITTLE GIRL

Four sous worth in my glass.

PAPA COLOMBE

It's for you?

LITTLE GIRL

No, it's for Mama who's got a cold. This is the only thing that calms her. Thanks. (she leaves)

BAZOUGE (calling)

Papa Colombe.

PAPA COLOMBE

Mr. Bazouge—You want?

BAZOUGE

A glass of the usual. (Papa Colombe serves him)

BEC-SALE

Ah, sonofabitch! (he bursts out laughing and bangs his fist on the table.)

MES-BOTTES (coming in from the other room)

Hello, my friends.

BEC-SALE

Give me a minute now! I've had a revolution. Freaky spendthrift taking a siesta—on the grass like a cow? Twenty, right? There follows—major thrust Twenty-three glaziers. Three cows, twenty-six, three flunkeys—twenty-nine—Three blind men, then eighty dozen. I'll bet a year for the Republic.

MES-BOTTES

You're washed up, my old friend.

BIBI

Well! I owe a round later on. (to Mes-Bottes) As for you, where are you coming from?

MES-BOTTES

From the side room where we were weighing iron joists—. The boss left, and I'm profiting from that to see if it's raining. Damn Papa Colombe! He's getting bigger. Now, he wants a billiard parlor.

BEC-SALE

By Jove, with what he steals from us. So, you've been working the last two weeks, have you?

MES-BOTTES

Oh, I believe you. I did three days in an hour.

BIBI

Exactly three days more than me. You're luck to be able to—get some money. That's what's annoying the best Saturdays of the month, the big pay days, like today—can't touch it. Me, I'm bored by it.

BEC-SALE

You don't want to work and get paid all the same. (laughing)

MES-BOTTES

Now that would settle the social question. Papa Colombe, Three Cognacs.

PAPA COLOMBE

Here we go. (he serves them. Mes-Bottes sits down)

BEC-SALE

Huh! This crook of a Papa Colombe. Is he going to make his butter today!

BIBI

In an hour they'll crush you at your counter. There's more than one whose wife's been waiting and they push you out the door with an empty pocket.

PAPA COLOMBE

I don't complain. Business is good.

BAZOUGE (calling)

Papa Colombe, a glass of the usual.

(Papa Colombe serves him.)

BEC-SALE (looking at Bazouge)

That makes three. Damned morning! Must work give up its share?

MES-BOTTES

Say, friends, just now I met Madame Coupeau.

BEC-SALE (pointing to Lantier)

Hush!

MES-BOTTES

Heavens! He's here, that individual. I didn't see him. Well, what difference does it make? He's angry with Coupeau but that doesn't prevent me from talking about them.

BIBI

In that case, what about Coupeau?

MES-BOTTES

Oh, my friends. A true conversion. Hell—it was time to stop. They aren't making any weddings like before in the shop. You remember? Coupeau ended the shop by drink. But when he saw himself in a dirty hole dying of hunger, with his daughter who's developed a taste for coquetry, and his wife who's lost her taste for work: then he swore to drink no more.

BIBI

And he's keeping his oath?

MES-BOTTES

Why, yes! Here it is six days that he's gone to the workplace with regularity. And not one drop of liquor.

BEC-SALE

Not possible! That's something you no longer see. (reaction by Lantier who has heard without seeming to)

MES-BOTTES

By Jove! I was telling you I'd met Madame Coupeau. She was really happy. (Lantier listens) She's counting on her fingers the money he's going to bring her this evening. Six days at seven francs makes forty-two francs.

BIBI

Holy cow! He'll have something to settle.

MES-BOTTES

And it seems it comes in handy. She's waiting for the money to eat this evening.

BEC-SALE

We knew that. No more—meat in the buffet. Never mind! Coupeau's wrong to scorn his friends. When he drank a bit from time to time it didn't poison him.

MES-BOTTES

Absolutely. To your health.

BAZOUGE (going to pay at the counter)

Papa Colombe. Three glasses of the usual. (he leaves. Bibi, Bec-Sale and Mes-Bottes continue to speak in hushed tones. Lantier approaches the counter.)

LANTIER (in a low voice)

Papa Colombe.

PAPA COLOMBE

What, Mr. Lantier?

LANTIER

You're certain he passes your house every day?

PAPA COLOMBE

Who's that—Mr. Coupeau? Oh, absolutely certain. I told you, I see him pass on the sidewalk at 6:40. In ten minutes he'll pass by.

LANTIER

Thanks. (he's kept his paper and continues to read standing up.)

MES-BOTTES (continuing in a low voice)

It's as I tell you. Madame Poisson has taken the shop from Madame Coupeau and set up a -confectionary business with an inheritance her husband has received.

BEC-SALE

And it's that spy of a Lantier who devours—the shop.

MES-BOTTES

Exactly. He's nourishing himself on sweets. He's all sugar. That fattens him.

BIBI

Damnation! Now there's one who goes from the brunette to the blonde and from the blonde to the brunette. What a profession!

BEC-SALE

But the husband?

MES-BOTTES

The husband? Hell! He's still chasing after his position as a cop. That keeps him busy. (all three laugh)

BEC-SALE (pointing to Lantier)

Enough gossip. I think he's sniffed us. (raising his voice) Hey, Mr. Lantier. It no longer says anything, your paper.

MES-BOTTES

(pretending to notice him) Heavens, Lantier. Hello. (they shake hands) What's new in politics?

LANTIER

Stupidities! Always the same thing. I was reading the court cases. A funny story. (Poisson enters and comes forward slowly, listening) Imagine, a husband who surprised his wife with a boy friend

MES-BOTTES

And he did her business?

LANTIER

Not at all. He's been made to give a note for a thousand. Very nasty, that.

BEC-SALE (elbowing Mes-Bottes)

Ah, exactly. The husband!

MES-BOTTES (offering his hand to Poisson)

Hello. It's great. Did you hear the story of the husband who—?

POISSON

Yes.

MES-BOTTES

As for me, I would have jumped on the—boyfriend. And you?

POISSON

Me? I don't know. I'd have to see. (to Colombe) Two vermouths. (slaps Lantier on the back and leads him away)

BIBI (to Mes-Bottes)

What would he have done? He would have offered him a round. Look. (they continue to talk)

POISSON (to Lantier)

Very well, Auguste. It's my wife who sent me. Your place was set, but from the moment you can't we're going to eat without you.

LANTIER

It's because I have some business.

POISSON

Exactly, my wife said: "Go see if the business is over and inform me."

LANTIER

No, the affair isn't over, but it's going well. You can tell her it's going well.

POISSON

What business is it?

LANTIER (hesitating)

What business? (excitedly) Oh, a meeting with a hat merchant. A situation worth a thousand francs.

POISSON

Superb. (gives his hand a tap) In that case, goodbye.

MES-BOTTES

Heavens! The husband is the one who's leaving. I bet he came on an errand from Madame. (stopping Poisson) Goodnight, Mr. Poisson.

POISSON (leaving)

Good night.

MES-BOTTES (watching him leave)

Go on! So much the better; he's still passing under the doors.

PAPA COLOMBE (to Mes-Bottes)

Say there, your boss is coming in through the side door.

MES-BOTTES

Ah, Screw it! I'm back to work. Later friends. (he leaves by the street door.)

BEC-SALE

He's good, Mes-Bottes. Till later! We haven't got a sou!

BIBI

And Papa Colombe has cut off the credit. Are you coming to the little man who coughs?

LANTIER (examining them, aside)

They have to go. (to Bed-Sale and Bibi) Say there, would you do me a favor?

BIBI

What is it?

LANTIER

It bores me to be angry with Coupeau. Now's the time he passes by. And wait! Here's the door on the boulevard. I'll pay for a lunch if you'll bring him in. I can make peace. It causes me too much pain when I'm angry with a friend.

BEC-SALE

A lunch! Accepted! Any time for friendship.

BIBI

And then we are going to see the head of Coupeau before the liquid. (both leave)

LANTIER

Papa Colombe?

PAPA COLOMBE

If you please, Mr. Lantier?

LANTIER

Four glasses of the best.

PAPA COLOMBE

There! (he pours four glasses aligned on the counter.)

COUPEAU (in the doorway, led by Bed-Sale and Bibi)

I tell you I don't want to go in.

BEC-SALE

They won't eat you, after all.

COUPEAU

My wife's waiting for me. I am already late. No, I won't go in.

BIBI

You've really got a minute.

BEC-SALE

I repeat to you that someone wants to see you. A fine business for you. A capitalist, an ambassador.

COUPEAU

Come on! One word, I am willing enough, then I run! Where is he, your capitalist?

LANTIER (advancing, hand extended)

What? You didn't guess?

COUPEAU

You! (to the other two) You knew! I don't like bad jokes.

LANTIER

You flee us. It's really necessary to tell you stories. Look, Coupeau, we can't always remain angry?

COUPEAU

I'm not angry with anybody. I do what pleases me, that's all. As I am happy now, I'm arranging for that to continue.

LANTIER

Then you're going to drink with us?

COUPEAU

Oh! As to that, never!

LANTIER

You see—it's already poured.

BEC-SALE (ironically)

He can't. His wife has forbidden him.

COUPEAU

Oh! My wife has forbidden me.

BIBI

Yes, Madame will beat him. (other customers hearing this laugh)

COUPEAU (stung)

My wife will beat me. We'll see about that.

BEC-SALE (ironically)

She's waiting for him. And it's even luckier that she doesn't wait for him at the factory door to sweep his pay away from him.

COUPEAU

Sweep away my pay! (tapping his vest—) The money is there. It's mine. I'm the one who earned it.

LANTIER

Are you a man? Yes! Will you swallow that for me? You won't die of it.

COUPEAU (hesitating, then deciding)

Quite so. Just to rid myself of you. To your health.

BEC-SALE (taping on Coupeau's vest)

Then the monacos are there!

COUPEAU

Yes, my old friend, forty-six francs—and hard-earned ones—flatter oneself. The rest of you are joking, but if you knew the pleasure that this gives me to bring it to my wife. It's true, she's waiting for me, that poor Gervaise.—Bye.

LANTIER (aside)

What! He's leaving?

BEC-SALE

You're running away. Well, you are nice! What, you've got dough and you don't give your friends in return the politeness they gave you.

LANTIER

Why, no, let him go. (paying) Papa Colombe, here's your money.

COUPEAU (stopping aside)

Ah, he's the one who pays.

BIBI

You must really have become good and drunk.

COUPEAU (returning to the counter)

Papa Colombe. Double that for me. It's my turn. (Papa Colombe fills the glasses)—But you are right. One politeness deserves another. To your health. (they clink glasses and drink)

LANTIER (putting his glass down)

That's numero uno.

COUPEAU (very gay, paying)

It's only Papa Colombe who disguises his vitriol that way. (he sniffs—the glass) Now there's an odor for you. Ah—Holy cow—it's nice all the same because it's a long while since I've stuck my nose in it.

LANTIER

Right! You, a water drinker! When one thinks that before you emptied a half decanter of brandy without taking a breath!

COUPEAU (flattered)

It's not for me to boast I had a strong wind.

LANTIER

I've seen stronger than you.

BEC-SALE

Truly?

LANTIER

Yes, in England. A sailor who drank a dozen glasses of brandy while they counted them off.

BEC-SALE (with admiration)

Not possible!

COUPEAU

With that, it's difficult. I bet I can do more.

LANTIER

I will take that bet. What are we going to bet?

COUPEAU

Whatever you wish. Twenty sous.

LANTIER (disdainfully)

It's worth more than that. Let's bet twenty francs.

COUPEAU

Twenty francs. It's all the same to me.

LANTIER

Papa Colombe. Add eight glasses.

BEC-SALE

Jesus! That's something to see!

COLOMBE (to Coupeau)

The gentleman is served.

BEC-SALE

Then release your chubby baby! You look like a nursemaid.

COUPEAU

It's true this bag is heavy. (he places it on the ground)

LANTIER

I am counting and not very fast. One—two—three—four—five—six—seven (as he counts, Coupeau drinks) you've lost. We're up to seven and you've only drunk six.

COUPEAU

My revenge.

LANTIER

I don't want to steal your money. You don't have luck—today.

COUPEAU

Ah, you refuse. There's twenty francs. (he gives them to him)

LANTIER

Listen, I'll make you double or nothing.

COUPEAU

That works. (all four sit at the table on the left. Papa Colombe brings a liter and six more glasses that Coupeau drinks.)

BEC-SALE

And your old lady?

COUPEAU (completely stoned)

Ah, leave me alone!

LANTIER (turning)

Twenty. (they laugh.)

COUPEAU

Mine. (he turns) Ten. Drowned. But I still have to pay for a round. Papa Colombe, give us something.

MES-BOTTES (entering)

What! Coupeau here! And beautifully lit up from what I can see.

COUPEAU (to Lantier, who gets up)

You're going?

LANTIER

Yes, I've had enough.

COUPEAU

In that case, you are not a man!

BIBI

You're leaving us.

BEC-SALE

You're making Charlemagne.

COUPEAU

Let him go, then. We don't have any need of him.(he drinks and snickers with Bec-Sale)

LANTIER

That's no longer my sort of thing, you see. When it gets nasty, I prefer to retire. Give me another paper. (he sits down and pretends to read.)

MES-BOTTES (standing aside)

Would Virginia have anything to do with this? (after a moment Gervaise can be seen prowling around the door. She appears in the doorway, hesitating. Mes-Bottes notices her.) Madame Gervaise.

(During the following, customers fill the bar)

GERVAISE

My God! I will never dare!

MES-BOTTES (aside)

Poor woman! (aloud) What do you want, Madame Gervaise?

GERVAISE

Ah, it's you. If you knew. I've been at the door for a quarter of an hour. In the past, I'd rather have been cut to pieces than enter here. And here I am! And here I am.

MES-BOTTES

For sure this is not the place for a woman.

GERVAISE

I've got to go in since my husband is here. I want my husband. (she heads towards Coupeau)

COUPEAU (seeing her)

Heavens! It's you! Oh! This is no joke, for goodness sake!

GERVAISE

It's here I must come to find you. After all your promises,

COUPEAU

I'm going to tell you, it's the comrades.

GERVAISE

I've been waiting for you for two hours. And not seeing you return I went to the work site. It was by chance that I had the idea of looking here, in passing. Let's go. Come!

COUPEAU

I can't stand up. I am pasted. Oh, no kidding.

GERVAISE

What have you done with your pay?

COUPEAU

My pay? They only pay on Monday.

GERVAISE

You lie! I saw your boss.

COUPEAU

I'm going to explain to you.

GERVAISE

Give me your money. I want it.

COUPEAU

Ah, in the end, you bore me. I've spent my money.

GERVAISE

Mercy on us! It's over. Now we've fallen back and we'll never rise again this time. And there I was, counting the hours, and I had promised money everywhere in the neighborhood.

COUPEAU

To Chaillot with the creditors!

GERVAISE

And you want to know what I say to you? I haven't eaten all day. I was waiting for bread. Let's go. Come on.

MES-BOTTES

Damnation! Go with her, since she's hungry—this woman.

COUPEAU (trying to rise)

I can't. (to Gervaise) Sit down for a minute, If you are going to make a scene where will that get you?

GERVAISE

I'm hungry, do you hear?

COUPEAU

Drink a cup. That nourishes.

LANTIER (who has risen)

A little cup will do you good,

GERVAISE (recognizing him)

You! Ah, I understand.

LANTIER (to Gervaise)

I told you plainly that I would remember.

GOUGET (entering, to Mes-Bottes)

So this is where you have work, do you?

COUPEAU

Don't be stupid. You've got troubles, Swallow this for me. You won't have them anymore. (he presents a glass to her)

GERVAISE (with somber decision)

Indeed, you are right. It's a good idea. Like this, we'll drink the money together. (she sits down and puts the glass to her lips)

BIBI and BEC-SALE

To your health.

GERVAISE (after having drunk)

It's true. It warms you up.

GOUGET (noticing her)

Oh! The wretched woman! The wretched woman!

CURTAIN

ACT V (1868)
SCENE 8

A miserable attic room. In a corner a mattress thrown on the ground. A cabinet without drawers. An old table, A chair. A part of a mirror hung on a wall. Doors on the left and at the rear.

AT RISE, Gervaise is seated in the chair, eyes fixed, head in her hands. Nana has finished arranging her hair at the partial mirror on the wall.

GERVAISE (low)

Yesterday evening, the baker refused me bread. We've finished the crusts of the old one. But today—what to do ,where to knock? Nothing, I find nothing for the hour I've been there,—wracking my brains!—my head. Ah! I want to be dead!— Nana!

NANA

Mama!

GERVAISE

You haven't tried to borrow 100 sous from your boss?

NANA

Yes. But she said it isn't done at the factory.

GERVAISE

What are you doing there?

NANA

You see plainly. I'm fixing my hair. We don't even have pomade, and all I've got is an old ribbon that's all faded. Truly, we need to have philosophy. Ah, fine. Now my dress has a tear in it again.

GERVAISE (who has fallen back into her reflections.)

We still cannot die of hunger. We must eat. My God! My God!

NANA

Is this dress worn out enough? A real lace. You promised me one for my birthday, but go see if it's come! No—it can't go on like—like this.

(she leans on her elbows, breaking the thread with her teeth, giving way to small rages)

GERVAISE

Nana.

NANA

Mama!

GERVAISE

Your father has been at Sainte Anne since Saturday before last?

NANA

I don't know any more. He goes there every month now. Yes, it must be the Saturday before last that they took him before the Boule Noire. See, I have—shivers there. (she goes into the next room)

GERVAISE (in a low voice)

No, I cannot go to his former boss. He would kick me out the door. Ah, when there's no longer a man in the household, it's finished! A man always finds something.

NANA (coming back and going to the commode)

No question. But since Papa is mad, I'm still afraid he will massacre us when he's been drinking.—I've still got to fix something with this ribbon. (she makes a knot with ends of old ribbons)

GERVAISE

So you're going out.

NANA

For sure I'm going out!

GERVAISE

Where are you going?

NANA

Why, to take a stroll! It's Sunday. Oh, don't worry. I'll be back in time for dinner.

GERVAISE: (to herself)

Dinner with what?

NANA (just about to leave)

Heavens, Madame Boche.

MADAME BOCHE (to Gervaise)

Yes, it's me. You haven't forgotten that we are the eighth. And I am paying my little visit to the tenants. I'm coming from the Lorilleux. Now, they are exact! They pay—pay to the last penny. I'm bringing you your notice to vacate.

GERVAISE

My notice to vacate!

MADAME BOCHE

Hell! You owe two months, and you know that the landlord doesn't joke. He told me that if you don't pay this very day, he will be forced to expel you.

GERVAISE

I have no work. Coupeau is in the hospital.

MADAME BOCHE

That's what I told him. But what do you expect? He really needs the rent money. He'll kick you out the door.

GERVAISE

Well! He'll put us out the door. We're no worse on the street than we are here.

NANA

Forget it, Mama! Landlords always threaten, Now—there, it's done. (going to look in the broken mirror) Very stylish! I'm going to the Boulevard.

MADAME BOCHE (low)

Say, Nana Who's this old gentleman who came to ask for you?

NANA (low)

Hush! Don't mention him to Mama. (aloud) Till later. (she leaves)

MADAME BOCHE (aside)

On the contrary, I am going to speak to her about it. (aloud) Madame Gervaise, I have to warn you. Just now an old gentleman came here. It was Bibi who told me about it, I wasn't there—but for that he would have gotten a good reception! He asked about Nana. In the end, be careful.

GERVAISE

My God! That's all it lacked! That's good, I will watch.

MADAME BOCHE

Then you can't give anything to the landlord? Not even a partial payment.

GERVAISE (weeping)

But since I tell you I haven't got a sou!

MADAME BOCHE

Don't despair. Perhaps there's still a way to get you out of it.

GERVAISE

How's that?

MADAME BOCHE

By addressing yourself to your friends.

GERVAISE

To whom do you want me to address myself? To the Lorilleux, perhaps?

MADAME BOCHE

Oh, no! They are too tight fisted, those folks! But still you have acquaintances. Madame Poisson, for example.

GERVAISE

No. Not that one! Never! She triumphs too much in my former shop. You might say the more I suffer, the more it pleases her.

MADAME BOCHE

Don't think that! What a nasty idea!—But there are still other persons.

GERVAISE

Other persons! Yes, there's Madame Gouget. I no longer see them, neither her nor her son. I'd much prefer to die a hundred times on the pavement than to have recourse to them.

MADAME BOCHE

Ah, if you are proud, In the end—suit yourself. I will return tonight. (she leaves)

GERVAISE

What have I done to the good Lord that he makes me endure all this? Let's see, let's try not to lose my head. Got to eat! If I find something to sell. (she makes a tour of the room) Lady who embroiders on the corner will give me twenty sous. Not a—not an object. Nothing except the four walls, I sold even the wool of my mattress handful by handful. Coupeau drank it all. Oh, the black misery! Who can I ask? (the voices of the Lorilleux are heard) The Lorilleux. Come on, although it costs me.(she opens the door and calls) Mr. Lorilleux.

(Mr. and Mrs. Lorilleux enter. They both remain in the doorway)

LORILLEUX

What do you want with us?

MADAME LORILLEUX

Hurry up because we are going to inspect some work.

GERVAISE

I would like—I did a laundry and they didn't pay me—Because it's Sunday, and folks are in the country. They will pay me tomorrow.

LORILLEUX (low to Madame Lorilleux)

That's a little fib.

GERVAISE

So—I'd like. You couldn't loan me twenty sous?

MADAME LORILLEUX (aside)

There it is! (aloud) Twenty sous, holy cow!

MADAME LORILLEUX (low to her husband)

Now there's a spendthrift. Today she taps us for twenty, tomorrow it will be double. None of that.

GERVAISE

You would be doing me a great service.

MADAME LORILLEUX

My dear, you know quite well that we don't have money. We would gladly, naturally—

LORILLEUX

We'd always be glad too! Only when one cannot, one cannot!

GERVAISE

I will return them to you tomorrow morning, when I've received my laundry money.

LORILLEUX (shrugging)

Your laundry money. We're not unaware that you haven't worked for a long while.

MADAME LORILLEUX

My dear, we've paid our rent; we remain without a red penny- indeed, we ourselves are very embarrassed for this evening. And then, you see, it's your fault! We warned you a long time ago. You have to work and be economical. Till another time. Goodnight. (she leaves)

LORILLEUX

Yes, till another time. Goodnight. (he leaves)

GERVAISE (bursting into tears)

My God! All abandon me. (she falls overwhelmed into a chair. The door opens and Virginia appears. She watches Gervaise weeping for a moment)

VIRGINIA

Hello, Gervaise.

GERVAISE (rising)

What do you want with me?

VIRGINIA

I learned you were all in pain, and I came to see what can be done for you.

GERVAISE (proudly)

Thanks. I don't want anything from anybody. Leave me alone.

VIRGINIA (in a soft tone)

Don't cry like that, No question things look black. I know that you no longer can find work anywhere, and I came to propose to you a little work with the idea of rendering you a service. Once a week if you would come to my place to clean the shop.

GERVAISE

To clean, to clean the floor.

VIRGINIA

That doesn't suit you. At your ease! Think that you have no one to count on. Everyone has distanced themselves from you. They won't give you credit for a sou in the quarter. The landlord is going to put you out on the street, and you will soon be completely alone, because Nana—

GERVAISE

Shut up! You're driving me mad!

VIRGINIA (always sweetly)

But, my dear, it's for your benefit that I am showing you your position. Still, if you had your husband—

GERVAISE

Oh, yes! If Coupeau were here, I'd feel saved.

VIRGINIA

But he's not here. And someone actually saw him at Saint Anne three days ago. The doctors told him he'll never get up again. Forgive me for bringing you this news.

GERVAISE

Lord! This is the final blow!

VIRGINIA (aside)

At last! In that case I'm going to have the power to tell her a nice time. (aloud) So there you are without any resources. A daughter who's going bad, a husband who's dying.

COUPEAU (entering with Mes-Bottes)

Greetings, everybody.

GERVAISE

Coupeau! (she throws herself in his arms) Ah, God of Gods! My poor husband!

VIRGINIA (aside)

She's not yet floored!

GERVAISE

But how does this happen?

MES-BOTTES

Here's the thing. This morning, went to Saint Anne to see him, I thought he was screwed—. Not at all. He was out of danger and the doctor told me: If you want to take him away, don't hesitate.

COUPEAU

Alas, I wasn't made to pray. (kissing Gervaise) All the same, I'm happy to see you again.

GERVAISE

And me, too!

COUPEAU

And Nana? Where is she so I can kiss her?

GERVAISE

Nana. (embarrassed) She went out.

COUPEAU

Ah. Heavens. It's Madame Poisson. Is everything well, Madame Poisson?

VIRGINIA

Very well. (aside) Come on! Role resumed!

COUPEAU

It's pleasant to find oneself at home. And in good health. For I feel like the New Bridge now. Ah, sonofabitch, how I am going to work.

GERVAISE (with sprit)

My God! Our misfortunes are over!

VIRGINIA

Then truly, here you are cured?

COUPEAU

Nothing more to be cured.

MES-BOTTES

On one condition. (to Coupeau) You know what the Doctor told you?

COUPEAU

Have no fear!

MES-BOTTES

If you put only a little glass of brandy in your body, you'll be done for. Oh, why—burned up like a bowl of punch. (he whistles) No more Coupeau!

COUPEAU

But he allows me Bordeaux, Old Bordeaux. As for Brandy, don't worry. If I'm the only one to enrich Papa Colombe he can shut up shop.

GERVAISE

You've said that so often.

COUPEAU

This time it's the truth. Thanks! I know what it costs. (shivering) If you think it's fun down there. Let's not think of that. I have an appetite. What is there to eat?

GERVAISE

Nothing.

COUPEAU

That's little!

VIRGINIA (quickly)

I am going to send you something, Mr. Coupeau. We really must help one another. (she leaves)

COUPEAU

Goodbye. (after Virginia has gone) So the money draw is like this, huh? Completely empty. Watch. You're going to go right away to my former boss and see if he wants me. As of tomorrow, I will be a roofer. And you will beg him to make me a little loan.

GERVAISE

That's it. I'm going there.

MES-BOTTES

And as for me, I'm running after Bibi. That scoundrel has owed me seventeen sous for the last six months. And if I find him, I will bring them to you.

GERVAISE

Let's go down together.

MES-BOTTES

Till later, my old friend.

GERVAISE

Don't be impatient. (aside, as she leaves) Perhaps, happiness is returning. (she leaves with Mes-Bottes)

COUPEAU (alone, looking around him)

Damn! It doesn't smell of opulence here! My poor Gervaise must have had lots of trouble. But I intend that from this hour she will be happy. (looking in the cupboard) Not a slice of bread! Complete famine. I arrived just in time. Holy Cow! What stomach cramps I've got.

(Madame Boche enters with a bottle in her hand.)

MADAME BOCHE

Hell, Mr. Coupeau, are things good?

COUPEAU

Very good, thanks.

MADAME BOCHE

Delighted to see you again. I'm bringing you this on behalf of Madame Poisson. A bottle of old Bordeaux. (she places the bottle on the buffet)

COUPEAU

That's not to be refused.

MADAME BOCHE

It's to water the dinner. Are you waiting for your wife to return with provisions?

COUPEAU

Surely! And we will drink to the health of Madame Poisson and to yours.

MADAME BOCHE

That's the thing. Goodbye (she leaves)

COUPEAU (alone)

There are still fine folks. We are going to celebrate my return. Nothing prevents it; I am really hungry. And Gervaise doesn't return. If I drank two fingers of wine to sustain me. That's not forbidden. On the contrary. (he takes the bottle) Damnation! This must be great, and what a smell! (He smells the bottle that he uncorks) Heavens! It's funny. I could be mistaken. (terrified)

What's this? Why, Hell. It's poison. It's brandy! I don't want it! I don't want it!

(he places the bottle on the table and flees to the other end of the stage.) Why did they bring me this bottle? It burns. The Doctor indeed told me: "One single glass and I am dead!" Never! Never! (comes closer) Look, I'm a man, This is stupid to tremble before a bottle. I won't touch it, that's all. Gervaise will go take it back.

(a silence)

After all, Doctors tell you a bunch of fabrications to frighten you. As if a little glass could kill a man. Now, that's a farce! (takes the bottle again.) By Jove, when one doesn't want to drink, one doesn't drink. Still, suppose I were mistaken. Perhaps, it is not brandy. (he tastes it) Indeed it is. (replacing the bottle, trembling) My God! They are leaving me alone and this bottle is here, and it's not necessary that I drink! Ah, stop! Enough of these lies. It's not going to kill you, it will make you live! Yes, I want to live! Gervaise! (he rushes into the next room with the bottle.)

GERVAISE

(entering, seeing him close the door) Well, what's wrong now? He'll know the bad news soon enough. His boss refuses to take him back. Good workmen are not lacking, he said! Useless to employ bad ones. (sadly) Come on, this won't be easy to get out of, not easy at all.

NANA (entering)

Ah, beautiful day. There are a lot of people on the boulevard. I earned a beautiful appetite. Nothing to eat?

GERVAISE

No!

NANA

What! Not even bread?

GERVAISE

No!

NANA

Yesterday, at least, there was some bread. In that case, good-night.

GERVAISE

Where are you going?

NANA (with effrontery)

I am going to dine!

GERVAISE

Wretched girl!

NANA

Oh, I beg you, Mama. Don't make a scene!

GERVAISE

You shan't leave! Your father is back; he'll know how to keep you here, he will.

NANA

Papa is here? I have no desire to be massacred. Goodnight.

GERVAISE

Coupeau! Coupeau, your daughter's leaving. Coupeau!

COUPEAU (entering, staggering, empty bottle in hand)

Huh? What? Who is it calls me? (Nana escapes and leaves the door open.)

GERVAISE (with terror)

Great God! He's drunk!

COUPEAU (throwing the empty bottle in corner)

That one's empty. I want another.

GERVAISE (recoiling)

We are ruined.

COUPEAU (in an access of delirium tremens)

This is nice; there are some whore houses here—a real party! And the music a bit nice. Now then, it's up with the lanterns in the trees with red balloons in the air! And they jump and they march! Fountains everywhere, cascades, singing water. Oh, you'd say it was the voice of a children's chorus.

GERVAISE

My God, he's gone mad!

COUPEAU (furious)

Still, traitress, all this! I'm on my guard. Silence, pack of rogues! Yes, this was meant to vex me. I'm going to demolish you, I am, in your whore houses! Oh, I'm burning, I'm on fire.

(falls screaming)

GERVAISE (at the door, calling)

Help!

MADAME BOCHE (coming)

What's wrong?

GERVAISE

Coupeau—look!

MADAME LORILLEUX (coming in with Lorilleux)

This is terrifying, he needs a doctor.

LORILLEUX

If you imagine that a doctor can do anything!

COUPEAU

Right! Rats! There are rats at this point in time. Will you leave me alone, villainous creatures! Heavens! That fat one who's biting me on the leg! Go away! He's devouring my hand. The rats, the rats—Save me!

MES-BOTTES (entering)

Ah, the poor fellow. (he wants to help him up)

COUPEAU

Don't you touch me! (looking into the void) My wife! How beautiful you are!

GERVAISE

I'm afraid! I'm afraid!

COUPEAU

You have a nice hair-do. Say, who's the guy hiding behind you? Damnation, it's him! The hat maker! (foaming) To the two of us, my younger brother! Must I drown you in the end! Pocket that! And at all! And at all! Ah, the scoundrel, he's killed me. It's full of blood. Ah! (falling in a heap on the mattress, where he dies)

GERVAISE

(on her knees beside him) He's dead!

ALL

Dead!

MES-BOTTES (picking up the bottle and sniffing it)

Brandy! (to Madame Boche) How'd this bottle get here?

MADAME BOCHE (low)

A bottle that Madame Poisson sent him. She told me it was Bordeaux.

MES-BOTTES (aside)

Ah, the bitch!

LORILLEUX (to his wife)

Bah! One drunk the less!

CURTAIN

ACT V
SCENE 9

The Boulevard Rochechouart. At the back the Montmartre Élysée. A wine merchant on one side, a bench on the other. It is night, the Gas is lit.

AT RISE, the music of a quadrille can be heard coming from the Montmartre Élysée. Passers-by cross the boulevard wrapped up all the way to the nose. Gervaise, in tatters, head enveloped in an old scarf unrecognizable, looks through the windows of the wine merchant's shop.

BIBI (stamping his feet)

Damned cold! A little snow is going to fall any moment.

BEC-SALE

That doesn't prevent one from amusing oneself.

BIBI (pointing to Gervaise who he doesn't recognize)

Not that one there! She's been watching people eat and drink at the wine sellers for half an hour. That must—make her feel empty. (Gervaise slowly goes away) Say, there, Bec-Sale, are you going home?

BEC-SALE

They kicked me out of my furnished room.

BIBI

Me, too.

BEC-SALE

And, as there's a wedding there, they are going to need some carriages.

BIBI

My old friend, life is turning bad on us. I haven't saved a sou, and that makes me think hard.

BEC-SALE

Like me.—I think that work is necessary.

BIBI

I didn't dare say it to you. Yes, I think it's time to work.

MES-BOTTES (coming out of the wine shop)

Heavens! You are here! you're taking the fresh air?

BEC-SALE

The fresh air is nice. My teeth are chattering.

MES-BOTTES

As for me, I'm coming from the marriage of Gouget, our boss. (pointing to the wine shop) Ah, my friends, it's good to be with honest folks. The boss has ended by marrying a good little woman that his mother selected for him. And they are laughing. They are happy. (with importance) You know, I'm putting myself straight.

BEC-SALE

Huh?

MES-BOTTES

Look at me. I am with the wedding, and I look clean. My half liter and no more!

BIBI (stupefied)

Not possible.

MES-BOTTES

The rest of you didn't see Coupeau die! Me, I saw it. Ah, damnation! That cured me. I would prefer to swallow a red hot poker than to go into Papa Colombe's for a drop. Dog of a Papa Colombe.

BEC-SALE and BIBI (together)

Dog of a Papa Colombe!

MES-BOTTES

And if you knew Coupeau's poor wife! Now there's one who

is really punished! A miserable woman that makes you cold in your spine. I'd prefer to spend ten hours a day at—the anvil.

BEC-SALE

In that case you are working.

MES-BOTTES

I should think so—from morning until night.

BIBI (to Mes-Bottes)

That animal of a Mes-Bottes. He's always been the worst! Tomorrow, we're going to the roofers!

BEC-SALE

That's agreed! And no more vitriol!

MES-BOTTES

Bravo, comrades! I wish that all the bad workers heard you and would do like you. (music from the Élysée. More Passers-by cross the boulevard. Virginia and Lantier appear and head toward the ball.)

LANTIER (to Virginia)

Suppose we were to go to the Élysée?

VIRGINIA

No, I beg you, let's go home.

LANTIER

What are you afraid of? Aren't we free until tomorrow?

BEC-SALE (low to the other two)

Hey! Yes, It's Lantier with Poisson's wife. I understand. Poisson must have left this morning. He went to his province to get his papers for his position as a cop—which he finally obtained.

MES-BOTTES (wanting to go toward them)

Those scoundrels!

BIBI (holding him back)

You're going to get yourself in a scandal. It's not your concern.

MES-BOTTES

The rest of you don't know. I've had it in my heart for a long time. (raising his voice) All the rogues are not in prison!

BEC-SALE

Will you shut up!

MES-BOTTES (coming forward again)

So the swine are having fun while good folk croak of starvation. (he plants himself in front of Lantier and Virginia.)

LANTIER

What's this man want with us? On your way, drunk.

MES-BOTTES

You do right not to be too familiar with me. Drunk, yes, my little one. I've been that but not any more, whereas, when one has committed evil deeds, nothing wipes that out.

LANTIER

Take care!

MES-BOTTES

I wanted to tell you that—to tell the two of you that for a long time. You can pass now.

(Lantier and Virginia distance themselves and go into the Élysée Montmartre) That eases me a little.

BEC-SALE

They don't seem to be at their ease. And to say that no one can arrest them, those scoundrels who know how to respect the law! If you give your neighbor arsenic, they cut your head off. But if you kill him by making him drink brandy, the cops take their hats off to you. There are poisons which are permitted. Won't a mishap fall from somewhere to crush these two no-goods? (Poisson enters and walks up and down)

BIBI (noticing Poisson)

Hey! There's Poisson.

MES-BOTTES

Huh?

BEC-SALE

Is he tracking the other two? No, he's too stupid.

BIBI

I don't trust these folks who don't talk. You never know what's going on in their head.

MES-BOTTES

Evening, Mr. Poisson.

POISSON

(drily) Evening.

MES-BOTTES

They said you went on a trip.

POISSON

I changed my mind.

MES-BOTTES

Ah! And what have you come here to do?

POISSON

I'm taking a walk.

MES-BOTTES

You choose a helluva time.

POISSON:

That's possible.

MES-BOTTES (aside)

He's not very friendly. For sure, something's wrong with him. (to Bibi and Bec-Sale) Say there, the rest of you, let me chat with this bloke.

BEC-SALE

Willingly. It's freezing. We're going to walk a little. (they go away)

(Poisson keeps looking to the right and left)

MES-BOTTES

Mr. Poisson?

POISSON

What?

MES-BOTTES

It's cold as a wolf.

POISSON

You think so?

MES-BOTTES

Meaning, if we stay here we're going to be congealed. Would

you accept a warm wine?

POISSON

Thanks, I have business.

MES-BOTTES

There, at this wine seller's.

POISSON (after having looked at the Élysée)

There, I'd really like that.

MES-BOTTES

Then go ahead. After, you Mr. Poisson. (they go into the wine seller's shop)

(The orchestra plays Schumannn's *Rêverie*. Gervaise walks in slowly. Lantier and Virginia leave the Elysee and slowly come forward, talking.)

VIRGINIA

No, I much prefer to go home. I am not at ease.

LANTIER

Because we met that man? Truly, that's not reasonable. Your husband is far away and we don't have to fear him.

VIRGINIA

All the same—Let's go home!

LANTIER

Now our evening is spoiled!

(Gervaise approaches them and extends her hand as if taking an abrupt decision)

GERVAISE

Charity, if you please. I haven't eaten for two days.

(The old cloak that masked her falls and one sees her in tears, hair all white.)

VIRGINIA (recognizing her)

Gervaise!

GERVAISE

Virginia!

VIRGINIA (explosively)

She's begging! She's begging! See that, Lantier, she's begging!

LANTIER (wanting to pull her away)

Come on, It's no use.

VIRGINIA

No, no. I'm no longer in a hurry now. I want to stay.

GERVAISE

Have pity.

VIRGINIA

Why, don't you know that since that day at the wash house, I've—watched for your ruin! Finally, I am avenged.

GERVAISE

She frightens me. (to Lantier) But you, you—?

LANTIER

I don't like scenes.

(Poisson appears)

VIRGINIA

I've taken everything from you. You've no longer got a thing. And I'm not afraid of anybody.—I love him.

(Poisson has come closer and raises his arm, holding a knife.)

POISSON

You love him? Take that. (stabs her)

VIRGINIA (falling dead)

Ah!

POISSON (taking Lantier by the collar, pushing him onto the wings, where he stabs him)

As for you!

LANTIER (off stage)

Ah! Gervaise, Great God! (she staggers and falls onto a bench. Cops rush in. Mes-Bottes, Bibi, and Bec-Sale enter as the cops take away Virginia's body and lead off Poisson)

MES-BOTTES

What's it all about?

BEC-SALE

The husband stabbed them both.

MES-BOTTES

At last. There is a good God!

BIBI (laughing, to Bec-Sale)

And he wanted to work in the station house. He's there now!

(all three leave. The snow falls)

GOUGET (coming out of the wine seller's shop.)

The people are moving away—a woman faints, dying. (recognizing Gervaise) Gervaise! Gervaise!

It's me, Gouget!

GERVAISE

You! I see you again before I go. Ah, how I thank the Good Lord!

GOUGET

I am going to find help.

GERVAISE

Useless. Don't pity me. My misfortunes are over. You see, I'm smiling. He was right,—the day of my wedding?

GOUGET

Who's that?

GERVAISE

The man! There are women who are really happy when they are carried off. Oh, yes, I am really happy.

GOUGET

Why it's a crime to leave you like this.

GERVAISE

Listen, Mr. Gouget, I can tell you this now. I am no longer offending anyone. I've always loved you. (she dies)

GOUGET

Poor creature.

MES-BOTTES (entering in the midst of a group)

Yes, he did well! If I were a judge, I would acquit him.

(seeing Gervaise's cadaver) Gervaise, dead!

BAZOUGE (entering)

A dead woman! The washerwoman! (he kneels near her.) You are cured of misfortune. You will rest at last. Go bye-bye, my beauty.

CURTAIN

ABOUT THE AUTHOR

Frank J. Morlock has written and translated many plays since retiring from the legal profession in 1992. His translations have also appeared on Project Gutenberg, the Alexandre Dumas Père web page, Literature in the Age of Napoléon, Infinite Artistries.com, and Munsey's (formerly Blackmask). In 2006 he received an award from the North American Jules Verne Society for his translations of Verne's plays. He lives and works in México.

www.ingramcontent.com/pod-product-compliance
Lightning Source LLC
LaVergne TN
LVHW041616070426
835507LV00008B/273